The Power of Benchmarking

by

Leonard Lane
Managing Director, Fung Academy

ISBN-10: 0998166588

ISBN-13: 978-0-9981665-8-2

Set in Century 12 Point
Design consultation: LaPointe Illustration
www.CatherineLaPointe.com
Printed in the U.S.A.
Deposited in the Library of Congress

Lexingford Publishing LLC
New York   San Francisco   Hong Kong   Ottawa
www.lexingfordpublishingllc.com

Author's Note

Let me be frank.

Of the thousands of available books on business, management, marketing and so forth, only a mere handful deal in depth with benchmarking. In fact, you are now holding perhaps the most thorough discussion of benchmarking in existence.

I write this not to impress you, but rather to emphasize the rare learning experience that lies before you in these pages. The seventeen chapters of *The Power of Benchmarking* have as their goal to make you a well-informed and highly adept practitioner of this vital business skill.

Please take one more sustained look at the cover of this book. You see there a rock with a ledge, or "bench," carved into its side. The important thing about this bench was that it was absolutely level, within the limits of the early surveyors. A sighting instrument—usually an iron rod—could be set on the bench. A surveyor could then look along that straight edge to make spatial sense of everything that lay within his view. You can imagine the value on hilly terrain of having a straight line of sight as the basis for land measurement, maps, and proof of "which way the water flows" for farming purposes.

Now take that concept (found, by the way, on every populated continent, especially Europe and Asia) and apply it as a metaphor for business benchmarking. The enormity of the concept is profound: you are "carving out" of your known world (your company, let's say) a line of sight to help you interpret the unknown world beyond—and to learn from it. You want to escape the tangle of anecdotes, competitive biases, and insular prejudices in order to "see straight" into the external world that surrounds your business and, in large part, determines its success or failure.

   The Power of Benchmarking shows you step-by-step, with what I believe to be the best examples from the last three decades, how to "mark" or pay attention to what you are able to perceive, thanks to the "bench" or sight-line you can create within your firm. In a literal sense, you will be using *what you know* as a lens to discover what you *need to know* to shape the future of your enterprise. What's more, you are performing this valuable exploration free from the obscuring factors of internal company politics ("what the boss wants"), and company traditions ("we've always done it that way"). Benchmarking, carried out with care, will uncover truths—even uncomfortable truths—that can help you plan for profitability, hire and deploy human resources, and strategize for optimal influence in your marketplace.

   So, in a phrase, prepare to "see straight" using the benchmarking techniques taught here. I welcome your questions, comments, and experiences through contact by means of my publisher, *www.lexingfordpublishingllc.com.*

   Leonard Lane
   Managing Director, Fung Academy
   The Fung Group
   Hong Kong
   June, 2017

Dedication

To the Fung Group Employees across the world who everyday strive to excel in a globally competitive market.

Preface

We are fortunate to live and work in an era where information is plentiful and, in fact, growing exponentially in its volume, complexity, and accessibility.

Therefore, let me begin with a reason for you to embark on your benchmarking journey with a question many of you have asked: 'I wish I could understand how my competitor is able to achieve growth in this turbulent white water business environment? Where and how do I get the data (knowledge) and then turn it into actionable information?'

In addressing these questions, context is important, so let's start with some history. Futurist David Russell Schilling recently summed up the burgeoning nature of knowledge: "Buckminster Fuller created the 'Knowledge Doubling Curve'; he noticed that until 1900 human knowledge doubled approximately every century. By the end of World War II knowledge was doubling every 25 years. Today things are not as simple as different types of knowledge have different rates of growth. For example, nanotechnology knowledge is doubling every two years and clinical knowledge every 18 months. But on average human knowledge is doubling every 13 months. According to IBM, the build-out of the 'internet of things' will lead to the doubling of knowledge every 12 hours."

Here's the key point—you have *access* to far more information than ever before. At the click of key or two, you can draw upon massive stores of data.

What you do with that data is paramount. Arriving at useful information for your company involves making *meaning* out of a wealth of raw bits and bytes. Useful information is what you seek above all in benchmarking: *the comparison of the nature and quality of an organization's policies, products, programs, strategies, and processes with standard measurements or similar measurements of its peers, including out-of-industry comparisons.*

Not that useful information is always easy to come by. Competitors do not usually volunteer closely-held information about their core competencies and areas of expertise. In fact, this book is largely concerned with practical and ethical ways to obtain useful information external to your organization and then apply it for the improvement, even the transformation, of your company.

The intellectual work involved in benchmarking is akin in many ways to the famous sleuthing of Sherlock Holmes. The goal of such detective work is not merely to collect information already known to everyone in the industry but instead to make connections and inferences that reveal the true "secret sauce" at the heart of competitors' strategies.

Those charged with such intellectual work must be prepared for surprises both happy and unhappy. On the happy side are discoveries that can be directly imported into your own business practices with short- and long-term benefits. An example is Facebook's discovery, by observation and investigation of other internet social media firms, of how to monetize its customer contacts in a way that did not drive away its members, a lesson that Skype apparently has yet to learn.

On the less happy side are puzzling and often frustrating revelations of disruptive technologies in the hands of your competitors—technologies that may be difficult for your company to acquire or contrary to its traditional culture. Benchmarking may reveal that your heretofore successful company is on its way to becoming an extinct dinosaur vis-à-vis competitors unless it leaps onto the learning curve with a commitment to survive and thrive through new paradigms and processes.

Leaders with a bent for learning and unbridled curiosity loved their work most of all when confronted daunting obstacles. But many organizations face the intense, wide-ranging activities of benchmarking with distaste, even loathing. In many cases, this resistance to benchmarking is due to a phenomenon known as "cognitive dissonance." When business professionals look without flinching into the realities that surround them in the outside world—market changes, currency issues, severe competition, unpredictable customer preferences, and the like—the "sound" of all that information can be dissonant indeed. It's not at all what they would like to hear, feel, or think about. It may contradict their fondest dreams for their company and themselves. It may reveal that they've been on the wrong path, in a business sense, for months or even years.

A particular source of cognitive dissonance is the siren song for companies that they are going to remain industry leaders by maintaining "competitive advantage," such as Amazon does through its continuous experimenting in all aspects of its business. It comes as dissonant "noise" to recognize that we no longer live in an era where can rest on the laurels of supposed competitive advantage. The exponential growth in both the science and application of chip technologies (and others) have humbled even the greatest names in commerce (Kodak comes to mind). Uber continually looks over its shoulder at rising competitors, just as Facebook constantly monitors the age groups to which it appeals. In an era of disruptive technologies, competitive *edge* trumps old-style competitive advantage.

A key finding of most conscientious benchmarking efforts is the realization that we can achieve competitive edge through perpetual innovation and a passion for excellence. Maintaining that edge means constant attention to our competitors, our enabling science and values, and the desires of our marketplace—in short, benchmarking to survive and prosper.

Given the potential resistance, are you prepared to take the risk of activating the benchmarking techniques covered in this book? You may risk being surprised, even appalled, by what you learn. But the greater risk is to choose ignorance of what benchmarking can reveal—in the famous words of F. Scott Fitzgerald in the conclusion to *The Great Gatsby*, we're rowing our "boats against the current, borne back ceaselessly into our past." Benchmarking offers the promise of looking unflinchingly at present business realities (even those we prefer not to see) and to be a useful window to likely developments in the future. It is our best defense against being borne back ceaselessly into our past as individuals or as companies.

Acknowledgments

This book is the product of a long and meaningful career that has been helped along by my colleagues, customers and students who have encouraged and motivated my thinking on the subject. To my colleague Arjan Singh for his tireless editing and, above all, a special thanks to the past and present colleagues in the Fung Academy who contributed their time, insights and support to this endeavor.

Table of Contents

Part I:

What is Benchmarking?

Chapter 1

Why Benchmarking?

In 2009, Research in Motion (RIM), creator of the Blackberry, owned 50% of the U.S. smartphone market. By early 2017, as this book goes to press, its share had plummeted to less than 1%!

How could the fortunes of a company have fallen so far and so fast? The answer lies not so much in what RIM did, as what it didn't do.

First, RIM failed to understand the changing decision process around who buys mobile devices in its key markets, the corporate and government sectors. Back in the late 1990s, RIM had built the company's reputation on having by far the best security for mobile devices. Starting off with two-way pagers, it had led the market into hand-held devices that could send and receive e-mails to and from corporate mail systems that were securely encrypted, while providing corporate IT department's central control over how to flexibly manage this flow of corporate information.

This understanding allowed RIM to grow and dominate these sectors of the early mobile market However, this was not to last. Ten years later, Apple launched the iPhone in the consumer market with less security, but far greater functionality. Apple quickly followed with the AppleStore and a revolutionary wealth of new consumer functionality. What RIM failed to understand was what it would take to continue to win in the expanding mobile market in the long-run. A strategic examination of the industry environment and the various competitors -- called *strategic benchmarking* - would have revealed that understanding the demands of consumers was the key to the whole market, rather than focusing on the limited demands of the corporate and government sectors.

Employees are also consumers and only want a single device for both home and work. As the supply of smart phones and their functionality accelerated, consumers would over-rule corporate decisions on what device they would use by making their own purchasing decisions.

Second, RIM took its eyes off its lead product, the Blackberry. When in 2010, Apple launched the iPad and created the tablet market, RIM decided it had to compete head-on. So rather than continuing to innovate around the Blackberry, RIM diverted key R&D and financial resources to creating and launching the PlayBook. It rushed to get this new product to market in 2011 and in so doing failed to include many key competitive features, like e-mail, calendaring, and contact management that Apple's product had, resulting in a serious product failure.

RIM had been dramatically unsuccessful in rigorously and realistically measuring where it stood versus the competition relative to key success factors, a process called *operational benchmarking*. It had needed to understand what resources key competitors like Apple were allocating to maintaining their drive into both the mobile phone and tablet markets. A good operational benchmarking analysis would have demonstrated that RIM's product resource allocations were way out of line. This would have shown that even if RIM had been successful in capturing significant market share and revenue in the tablet market, it was very likely that one of the growing number of competitors in the smartphone market would out-design and out-manufacture the Blackberry, which is exactly what happened.

Apple launched the iPhone with touchscreen, GIS, voice recognition and apps through the Apple Apps Store, Google introduced an open software solution and Samsung innovated around large screens, better understanding that voice calls are becoming less important and messaging and texting more important to consumers. With all this constant leading-edge development going on around the smartphone market, RIM could not afford to move its corporate attention away from the Blackberry to the PlayBook.

Now in 2017 with less than one fiftieth of the market share it had only 5 years ago, RIM faces additional issues needing operational benchmarking. Costs have become s major issues as it now has to compete against Samsung as the largest manufacturer of cell phones and its unparalleled low cost supply chain. Samsung's ability to survive its Galaxy 7 lithium battery crisis is testimony to the financial depth and product diversification of the company.

How could RIM have miscalculated so badly? Surely the analysis and observations described above are not so startling that RIM could have missed them so completely. And isn't RIM a company that spends millions of dollars every year on planning through many internal departments and outside consultants to prevent just this kind of blunder?

In actual fact, even some of the most momentous decisions of the company were made "on the fly." For example, a focus group of company executives was convened to name the prickly bundle of keys and wire that was the prototype Blackberry. Various suggestions were thrown out on the table. One branding consultant, a Californian amidst the VIPS of this Canadian company, remarked that "it looks like a blackberry to me." After a couple more hours of debate, a top leader at RIM said, "I like that blackberry name." It stuck. Only later did the American consultant learn that no-one around the Canadian table had ever heard of a blackberry. In Canada the fruit is called a gooseberry. So much for in-depth benchmarking, although the company never regretted the name they chose for their product.

In truth, the issues for RIM were at the most senior levels of management. RIM's management failed to agree who was their customer. Co-CEO and founder, Mike Lazaridis, saw it was the corporation, while Co-CEO Jim Balsillie and other senior management, the consumer.

What exacerbated the general miscalculation was a lack of an *effective benchmarking process* or system to make sure that these critical strategic conflicts around who is the customer and whether resources should be diverted aware from the company's world leading product could be openly discussed and resolved. Good but isolated benchmarking analysis isn't enough: any company, large or small, must have some sort of process to regularly and realistically identify the key success factors of its industry and measure how it stacks up versus the competition in terms of those key success factors.

These three topics--strategic benchmarking, operational benchmarking, and the benchmarking process--are the primary focus of the rest of this book. Strategic benchmarking is covered in Part II and operational benchmarking in Part HI. We begin the discussion of the benchmarking process in the rest of Part I and continue to address the benchmarking process throughout the rest of the book.

Denial Raises Its Ugly Head

But before we enter into the serious work of this book, we must face one issue head-on: If benchmarking is all the great things this book claims it to be, why is it ignored, partially or completely, by so many otherwise savvy business leaders? The answer, in the title of Richard S. Tedlow's best-selling book, is **DENIAL: *Why Business Leaders Fail to Look Facts in the Face—and What to Do About It*** (Portfolio, 2011).

According to Tedlow, the "culprit is abundantly clear: denial. Denial by financiers who pursued short-term gain while ignoring long-term consequences that were highly likely, if not inevitable. Denial by the banking and real estate industries that what goes up can come down. Denial by homeowners and consumers that the bills for goods bought on credit will someday come due. Denial by investors who convinced themselves, once again, that "this time, it's different." Denial by politicians and bureaucrats of inconvenient truths that did fit their free-market ideology. Denial even by swindlers whose Ponzi schemes could only end in disaster, not just for their victims but for themselves."

Denial has the unfortunate effect of killing benchmarking—or even the motivation to consider benchmarking. Once a company, work group or individual is convinced that there's nothing to learn from competitors and the external environment, there appears to be no reason to do the hard work of benchmarking. Why bother?

An Example of Denial

That question—"Why bother?"—can be ruefully answered now by Target Corporation. As described in extensive investigative reporting by *Fortune* (Jan. 15, 2015) and other business magazines, Target's greatest business gaffe in the history of the company was the direct result of denial of several kinds and at several levels within the organization. The facts of the disaster were thoroughly publicized: In 2013 Target attempted to create "Target Canada" by opening 124 stores—large, "Target-sized" stores—throughout that country. Less than 24 months later, Target CEO Brian Cornell closed that entire operation, with a resulting writedown for the company of $5.4 billion USD and a net loss from the Canadian expansion of more than $2 billion. "Our Target Canada business had reached the point where, without additional funding, it could not meet its liabilities," CEO Cornell blogged. "Simply put, we were losing money every day."

Analysis

Denial based on poor examination of location. Target acquired a massive, immediate footprint in Canada by taking over the defunct Zeller chain of department stores in 2011. In hindsight, Target executives wished they had examined more closely the reasons for Zeller's failure. In fact, as reported by Fortune, the Zeller locations were "dumpy, poorly configured for Target's big-box layout, and were in areas not frequented by the middle class customers Target covets." The allure of capturing massive square footage in one fell swoop across a country of 36 million people blinded Target leaders to the wisdom of "location, location, location."

Denial based on poor product selection and availability. Prior to making its bold move into Canada, Target certainly had plentiful anecdotal evidence that Canadians loved U.S.-based Target stores. Focus groups among Canadian snowbirds visiting Florida's many Target stores confirmed that these northern visitors loved the one-stop shopping at attractive prices for every typical domestic product, ranging from clothing to sports equipment to furniture to groceries. The company did not even have to spell out its name in U.S. ads. Simply the family "target" symbol said it all—the place to aim for when shopping.

But stocking 124 new Canadian stores to the level of quality, quantity, and price Canadians had come to love in the U.S. proved tricky. Target leaders had closed their eyes to major glitches in supply chains for distant Canadian stores, frequent tariff difficulties and delays, and a product mix geared specifically to a Canadian clientele. The result, evident particularly during the crucial Christmas shopping season, was a Target store in an off-the-beaten-path location with half-empty shelves. Word spread quickly among Canadian shoppers—"Don't bother." Most of these customers contrasted the fulsome variety and convenience of American Target stores with what they were being offered in Canada under the Target banner. The comparison was devastating for Target sales in Canada.

Denial based on underestimating the competition. In the U.S., Target had fared well against fierce competitors, especially Walmart. Target stores had an edge on perceived product quality, with not much difference in price. Pleased shoppers made a joke of pronouncing "Target" with a French twist—"Tarzhay"—to signal to friends that they were not above shopping for bargains, but simultaneously appreciated Target's more upscale shopping environment and sprinkling of top brands at cut-rate prices.

Walmart, which already had a well-established presence and pattern of profitability in Canada, was willing to go to the wall in price-point competition to keep Target from cutting into their market share. In the weeks leading up to Christmas, from 2013 through 2015, Walmart carried out a well-conceived media blitz that left Target in the position of an also-ran. The homegrown big-box store, Canadian Tire, undertook a similar if less extensive ad campaign. (Canadian Tire, for the uninitiated, sells a vast variety of hardware and domestic products. Tire sales, in fact, are only a small part of their business.)

Given these dependable alternative shopping locations—with shelves fully stocked to the breaking point with products chosen specifically for the Canadian shopper—it became an increasingly hard sell for Target to wean customers away to out-of-the-way, half-empty stores with no particular price advantage.

Target had fallen into denial based illusion of invulnerability based on its legendary U.S. success. While they recognized that their Canadian stores were experiencing a variety of problems, they felt that Canadian shoppers who loved U.S. Target stores would be patient while the company ironed out its wrinkles. Clearly, as CEO Brian Cornell admits, the company miscalculated. Canadians, it turned out, had a strong disposition to "buy Canadian" unless persuaded otherwise by an attractive, price-conscious shopping experience. There was no patience factor extended to Target as it slowly and awkwardly attempted to catch up with the market leaders such as Walmart and Canadian Tire.

Denial based on social consequences. Without overstating the case, it can fairly be said that terminating a U.S. Target employee or downsizing a particular store or region was considered "just business." Minimum-wage employees whose U.S. jobs with Target disappeared were expected to "disappear" in a way themselves—that it, to move on to another minimum-wage job, probably at a similar big-box stores. Obviously, Target leaders in the U.S. did not recognize the heightened social conscience of Canadian workers, many of whom had been suspicious of the economic giant to the south and, in some ways, the victims of U.S. corporate and governmental maneuvering to keep the Canadian dollar "cheap" in relation to the U.S. dollar and, hence, the buying power of the average, heavily-taxed Canadian perpetually low.

When the axe fell on thousands of Canadian Target employees at the end of the fiscal year in 2015, a shock wave rippled across that country verging on hate. In the majority of cases, Canadian workers had quit their jobs at other companies to accept Target's employment offer. They were left high and dry with Christmas bills in one hand and their pink slip in the other. Target had not only fouled its economic opportunities in Canada but had sullied its corporate name and reputation, making any later entrance to the Canadian retail market difficult at best. Canadian workers who perceived themselves to be "burned" by a U.S. giant guilty of poor foresight and planning would tell their stories of woe for decades to everyone they knew. Target in many Canadian quarters had become a four-letter word.

The Flipside of Denial

What could Target have done better in its Canadian foray? One is tempted to say "everything." The viability of old Zeller store layouts and locations could have been market-tested in advance. Target's ability to fill its shelves to U.S. standards could have been worked out in detail before "grand" openings of 124 Canadian stores. Product preferences of Canadian shoppers could have been determined, based on what they were buying at Walmart, Canadian Tire, and elsewhere rather than simply assumed to be the same as shopping choices in the U.S. Finally, the implications of firing thousands of Canadian workers in 124 failed Target stores could have been handled with greater sensitivity and compassion.

In short, the subtitle of Tedlow's book could have become Target's mantra and cautionary tale in entering the Canadian market: "Why Business Leaders Fail to Look Facts in the Face—and What to Do About It."

Chapter 2

Benchmarking in the Strategic Planning Process

To understand benchmarking, it is important to grasp the role it plays in the strategic planning process. It is almost impossible to conduct good benchmarking without relating it to the overall strategy of the company. Conversely, no good strategic planning process is complete without a solid benchmarking analysis.

A Framework for Strategic Planning

The starting point for any strategic planning process is a statement of the fundamental goal of the corporation. While a company strives to meet the needs of a variety of constituencies ·· employees, the local community, society at large ·· the most fundamental goal of the corporation is to maximize *shareholder* value.

The reason for this is simple: unless the company is earning a good return for shareholders, the shareholders will not continue to invest capital in the firm. When capital dries up, the corporation will find itself unable to meet the needs of employees to keep their jobs, to earn raises, and to be promoted. Nor will it be able to meet the needs of the local community or society, which needs investment in facilities and advancement of products and technologies for the greater good.

The phrase "shareholder value" was not coined by economist Milton Friedman, but is now virtually synonymous with his name and work. The point is worth making, however, that many modern companies have interpreted "shareholder value" in ways that Friedman never intended. These companies—among them, Amazon, Twitter, Facebook, and a host of others—understand shareholder value to be a long-term proposition, with "dividends" paid more in promises for future financial empires rather than in cash. The financial markets, and in particular the stock analysts of major investment firms, have largely embraced this extension—some would say departure—from Friedman's insistence on the primacy of shareholder value. Amazon in particular has had a long glidepath in its ultimate rise to be the "go-to" retailer of virtually everything that is sold on earth. Shareholders had to believe for several years that Amazon could accomplish what quarterly results seemed to refute.

Other companies such as Zappos have interpreted shareholder value more in a socially conscious context than in financial terms alone. For Zappos, the shareholder is best served by the company's involvement in projects dedicated to the amelioration of human suffering and the promotion of socially progressive causes. Company leaders argue that focusing exclusively on the low-hanging fruit of selling shoes and other apparel might produce superior quarterly results but would not be sustainable in a world where the "value" of a company is evaluated by shareholders in ways that go far beyond financial analysis.

Returning to the context of Friedman economics, however, Ford Motors has been a perfect example of the need to maintain shareholder value. For decades, Ford was one of the most paternalistic companies in America. The company has always striven to create a predictable, positive environment for employees, including regular promotions and pay increases and the avoidance of layoffs. The founder Henry Ford is famous for doubling wages to $5 a day and reducing the workday from nine to eight hours in 1913, with the result all his workers not only would put their all into their work, but could also afford to buy his product, the Model T.

In addition, when in 2008 the global financial crisis hit the U.S. economy, the whole of the U.S. automobile market, including Ford, went into a major recession. Twenty-five thousand UAW workers were laid off. The combined U.S. sales of the Big Three, Chrysler, Ford, and GM effectively halved from $8.1 million in 2007 to $4.6 million in 2009. The effect on the local community of Detroit was disastrous and the city is far from recovered even today. For Ford, the crisis has meant a major revamping of its products and realignment to what the market wants, especially in terms of fuel efficiency.

The second foundation of any strategic process is the recognition that *profitability* is the basic driver of shareholder value. Market share, low cost, and growth are all nice objectives, but they're only means to an end. Unless those and other accomplishments lead to strong profits for the shareholders, they will not be translated into a high stock price and a maximization of shareholder value.

There is a wealth of empirical and theoretical evidence demonstrating the close correlation between profitability and stock price, and it is not the purpose of this book to replicate those arguments. However, all of that evidence merely confirms something that is common sense to anyone who has ever owned his or her own business. You cannot take home revenue, growth, or market share at the end of the day; you can only take home revenue less cost, or profits.

The companies that have produced the strongest profitability and thus return to shareholders on a sustained basis tend to do three things very well.

First, they view the selection of the businesses in which the company competes to be a conscious, active decision which the company must make on a continuing basis. Well-run companies actively select the businesses they're in through acquisitions, research and development, joint ventures, product-line extensions, divestitures, and so forth. Companies which are not strategically managed tend to view the businesses they're in as a "given"; if they were in ten businesses a year ago, they'll be in the same businesses today. The strategic company may stay in the same set of businesses for a long period of time, but only because each of those businesses is pulling its weight and contributing to the overall corporate objectives, not because of inertia, as the flowchart indicates:

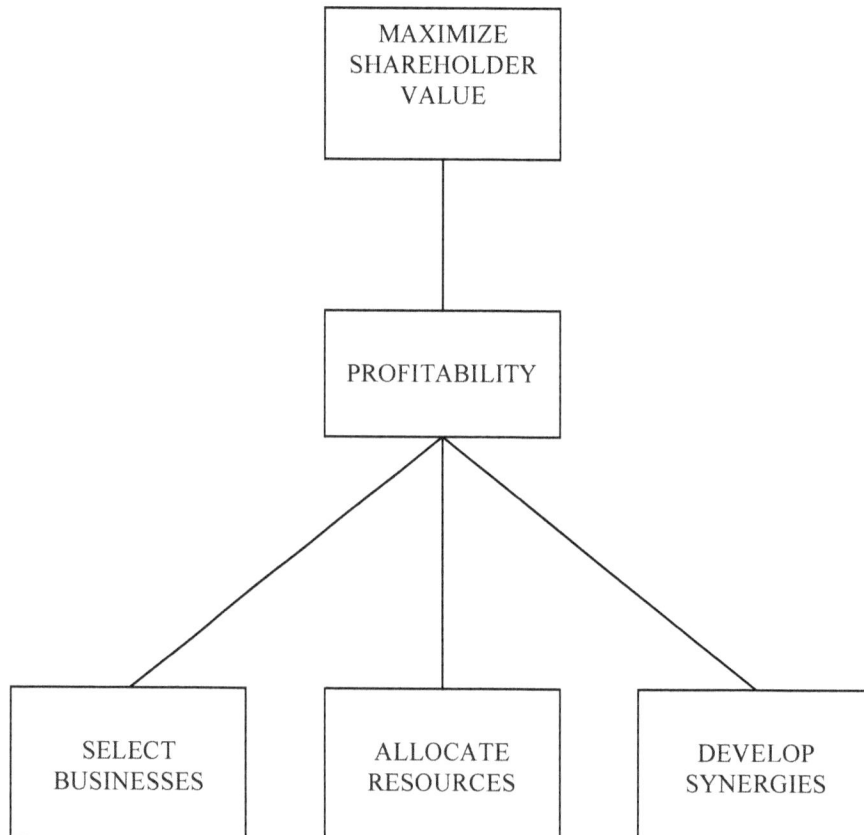

```
                    ┌──────────────────┐
                    │    MAXIMIZE      │
                    │  SHAREHOLDER     │
                    │     VALUE        │
                    └──────────────────┘
                             │
                    ┌──────────────────┐
                    │  PROFITABILITY   │
                    └──────────────────┘
                    ╱        │        ╲
                   ╱         │         ╲
         ┌──────────┐  ┌──────────┐  ┌──────────┐
         │  SELECT  │  │ ALLOCATE │  │ DEVELOP  │
         │BUSINESSES│  │RESOURCES │  │SYNERGIES │
         └──────────┘  └──────────┘  └──────────┘
```

A prime example of aggressive business selection is Reckitt Benckiser, a company that was created by the merger of UK-based Reckitt & Colman and the Netherlands-based Benckiser NV in 1999. The company is in the global health, hygiene and home products markets selling cleaning products, antiseptics and healthcare products. Right from its formation, it created a business model where it would centrally manage a very limited number of "power brands" for the global market and let local managers add local products if there were profitable. As a result, Reckitt has managed to maximize the value out of every brand it manages. Globally, it uses its knowledge how best to sell its power brands, especially with the use of line extensions - related products, or ones with slight change of formulation. Its power brands have consistently allowed it to grow year-on-year from sales of $5 billion in 1999 to $15 billion in 2013, or at a spectacular CAGR of 9% per year for the whole 14 years. Not surprisingly, its share price has outperformed all its nearest competitors, Unilever, Colgate and P&G.

Domino's Pizza (now simply Domino's) is another prime example of a company seeking to maximize its brand and positioning in the marketplace as a provider of urban food and food delivery, not merely "another" pizza company. Domino's in 2016 unveiled a special vehicle, engineered for them by GM, equipped with a heated locker and other amenities to ensure that food comes to the customer piping hot and indistinguishable from what might come straight from the kitchen at their favorite restaurant. Domino's bases its major strategy shift toward urban food delivery (not just pizza) on the premise that home-cooked meals are not a reality for the increasing numbers of residents in large and mid-sized cities. Domino's faced the hard reality that these residents are not going to order pizza night after night—but they may order from a Domino's menu that offers a wide variety of meals, with special vehicles to ensure restaurant-quality standards in terms of food temperature and delivery time.

The second concept fully understood by well-run companies is the need to actively and discriminately allocate resources among their various businesses. Unstrategic companies often follow a resource allocation rule of "everybody gets a little." If they're in ten businesses, and there is a certain amount of capital or strategic discretionary resources to spend, those resources get spread around the businesses in an even or proportional manner. *Strategic* companies follow a very different pattern. They may be in ten businesses, but they'll decide that several of the businesses have strong profit prospects, several have mediocre profit prospects, and several have limited potential. They will funnel the bulk of their strategic resources to the high potential businesses, some capital to the mediocre businesses, and almost none to the weak ones. These companies succeed in maximizing profitability by making sure they're not throwing good money after bad.

General Electric is an excellent example of a company that enjoys superior profitability through careful allocation of resources. G.E. identifies its winners, its mediocre businesses, and its losers. Then it funnels the bulk of its capital toward areas where profitable returns are likely to result. Not coincidentally, G.E. consistently outperforms its competitors and has enjoyed high profits despite being in some very competitive industries.

Another prime example of "spend-where-it-counts" use of resources is the publishing industry world-wide. Authors who sign a book with a major publishing house—a textbook on marketing, let's say—have the reasonable expectation (usually not stated in any contract from the publisher) that their book will receive high-profile exposure to the academic marketplace and sufficient advertising and promotional expenditures to give the book its best chance for financial success, both for the author and the publisher. What the author does not know, however, is that the same publishing company that signed their book may in the same month have signed several other marketing books targeting exactly the same academic marketplace. The relatively small advance given to the author (perhaps $5000 to $10,000) is 'chump change' to the major publishing company, as is the cost involved in preparing and publishing the book (perhaps $4 to $5 for a 200-page textbook that will sell for $70 to $80 retail). This arbitrage allows the company to sign several books that, unknown to the authors, *compete among themselves within the same publishing company* for marketplace prominence. As soon as the publishing company recognizes that one of the books it has signed is winning approval in the marketplace over the other books signed simultaneously, the lion's share of promotional expenditures from the publisher are immediately diverted to this "winner," with no further significant investment in signed books that didn't succeed as quickly or as well. Authors who complain that their book was just one among many signed in the same period by the publisher are told that nothing in the contract prohibited the publisher from simultaneously signing books, even if they competed directly against one another.

Third, successful corporations find synergies or linkages which cut across their various businesses. In other words, these companies develop skills which make the whole greater than the sum of its parts.

A prime example of synergy development is Apple, especially after Steve Jobs returned to the company in 1997. Firstly, he redesigned Apple's computing platform and launched the iMac in 1998. Jobs was a visionary and understood the need for consumers to have entertainment and information constantly at their fingertips. In so doing, he became a leader in creating today's mobile world through a series of products that were synergistically linked through image, functionality, operability and technology.

In 2001, Apple opened the first Apple retail store to showcase and sell its computers. The iPod was launched in the same year, followed by iTunes and the Apple iTunes Store in 2003. The iPhone was launched in 2007, followed by the Apple Apps Store and the iPad in 2010. All these products were linked, as well as other Apple creations like Apple TV and, very recently, the Apple Watch. They automatically work with each other, and all are supported by free telephone and in-Apple store experts, at the Apple Genius Bar. Apple's Stores have become the most profitable retail outlets in the world, generating a massive $18 billion and sales and an amazing 26% of Apple's profit margin. None of Apple's competitors come even close to the success that Steve Jobs created.

In building (or, in truth, leasing) "brick-and-mortar" stores in expensive mall locations, Apple took a considerable risk based largely on focus group information that customers didn't want to choose products or resolve product issues by difficult conversations with so-called "specialists" working customer service phone banks based in India and elsewhere. (This was the cost-saving alternative chosen by Dell and other competitors to Apple.) Apple dignified the role of store employees by installing a "Genius Bar" in each store, where customers could have their questions answered and problems solved by an Apple-trained customer expert. This service, importantly, was provided "within arm's length," not a continent away. The Apple "genius" (a term good for employee morale") had wide latitude in recognizing a defective Apple product and solving the customer's problem on the spot by replacing the flawed product. Word-of-mouth feedback was overwhelmingly positive from customers, many of whom were spending in excess of $1500 on a sophisticated piece of computer hardware they did not pretend to understand. The nearby presence of an Apple store with knowledgeable employees empowered not only to explain but to resolve any problems made the price of an Apple computer or other product a secondary consideration to the fact that customers could get the product to actually work for them—and had a nearby backup from Apple in case it didn't.

Another example of successful synergy development is provided by Proctor & Gamble. P&G competes in a wide range of consumer products including diapers, detergents, paper products, coffee, and so forth. Yet P&G really derives its strengths from a number of fundamental synergies which cut across the entire company: low network television advertising rates negotiated based on its overall scale of advertising across its product line; a leading-edge understanding of digital marketing; an excellent market research capability cultivated from years of experience in many different product areas; a strong distribution system through which the entire product line is channeled; and technological strength in certain types of products. For example, today P&G views digital marketing as simply "brand building" and not an isolated component of its campaigns. As a result, it started its ad campaign for Braun Shavers in the digital world and built it back into the rest of the marketing mix, rather than the other and traditional way around. Those strengths give P&G advantages which a competitor in an individual product area cannot replicate.

Conducting Strategic Analysis

In order to effectively *select businesses, allocate resources,* and *develop synergies*, a company needs to fully understand the strategic nature of its industry. That is why an *industry analysis* is normally the first step toward strategy development. Industry analysis is a systematic process for assessing the environment in which a business operates. As depicted on the flowchart on the following page, it includes fundamental analysis of the economic forces which shape an industry: the degree and nature of competitive rivalry, the power of customers and their purchasing behavior, the power of suppliers, barriers to entry, threat of substitute products and services, industry economics, government regulation, and so forth.

A Framework for Strategic Analysis

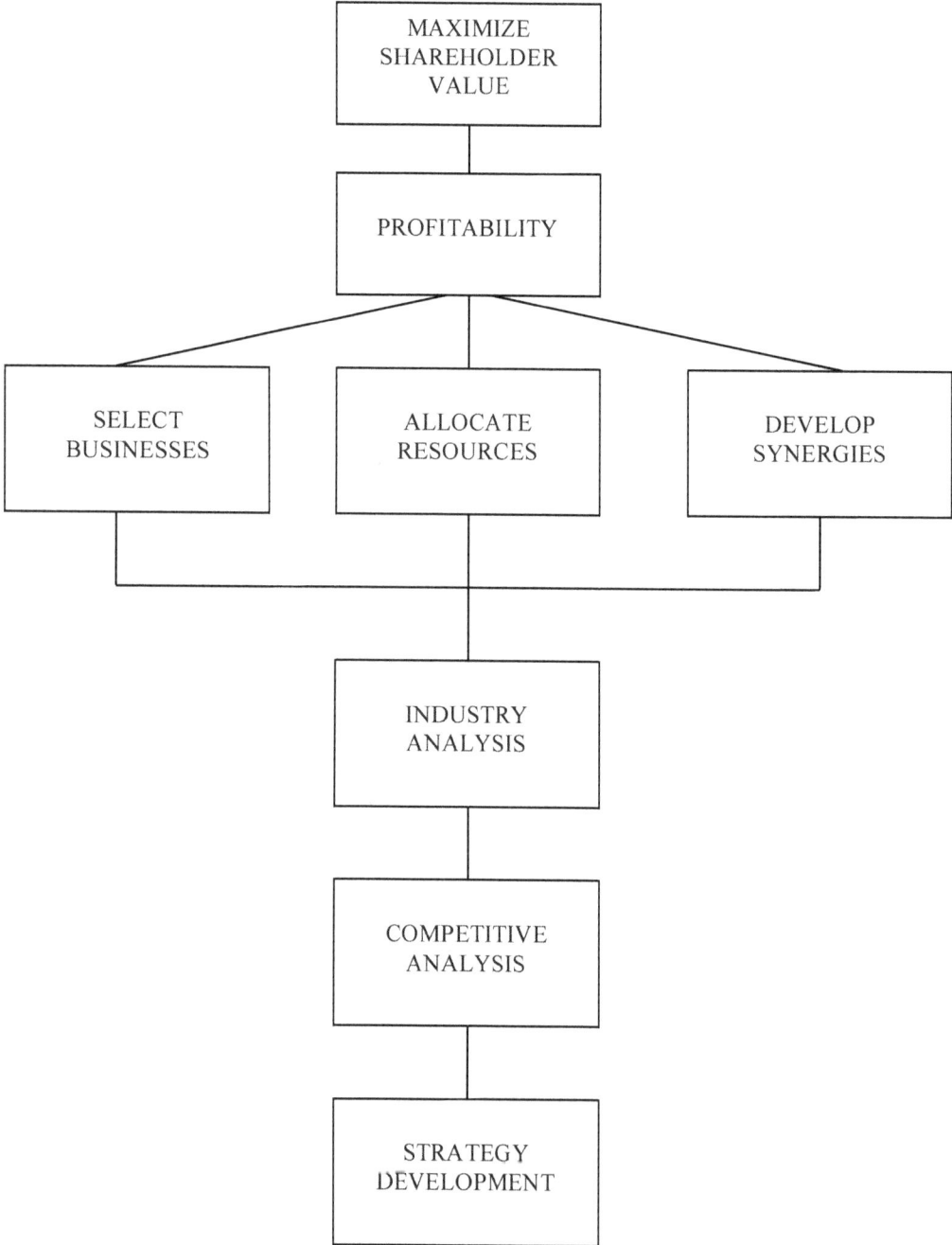

```
              ┌──────────────────┐
              │    MAXIMIZE      │
              │   SHAREHOLDER    │
              │      VALUE       │
              └──────────────────┘
                      │
              ┌──────────────────┐
              │  PROFITABILITY   │
              └──────────────────┘

  ┌──────────────┐  ┌──────────────┐  ┌──────────────┐
  │    SELECT    │  │   ALLOCATE   │  │   DEVELOP    │
  │  BUSINESSES  │  │  RESOURCES   │  │  SYNERGIES   │
  └──────────────┘  └──────────────┘  └──────────────┘

              ┌──────────────────┐
              │    INDUSTRY      │
              │    ANALYSIS      │
              └──────────────────┘

              ┌──────────────────┐
              │   COMPETITIVE    │
              │    ANALYSIS      │
              └──────────────────┘

              ┌──────────────────┐
              │    STRATEGY      │
              │   DEVELOPMENT    │
              └──────────────────┘
```

The goal of industry analysis is to answer two fundamental questions. The first is: How profitable is my industry likely to be on average, now and in the future? Some industries, because of the industry forces described above, are fundamentally more profitable than other industries. For example, an average competitor in the pharmaceutical industry earns far higher returns than the average competitor in the steel industry. A good industry analysis segments your market into a number of different sub-markets, and assesses the relative profit potential in the various parts of the industry. Obviously, all other things being equal, those portions of the industry with higher profit potential are more likely to merit investment of strategic resources.

The second question answered by a good industry analysis is: what are the key success factors in the industry? Is low cost the key success factor? Is a differentiated technology the only way to earn superior levels of profitability? Are sales and distribution the key? And how do the key success factors vary among the different sub-segments within the market?

In other words, an industry analysis tells you the profit potential, on average, of your industry, and the key leverage points that will cause some companies to out-perform the industry average while others do poorly. The computer industry has matured, and on average earns lower returns than it once did. But within that average, IBM and Apple consistently earn higher returns than many other players. Industry analysis permits us to attribute this success to the fact that their strengths fit the industry's key success factors more closely. (For detail on industry analysis, see this book's companion volume, *Developing Industry Strategies: A Practical Guide to Industry Analysis*).

Industry analysis is made extraordinarily difficult in some markets when customer preferences shift quickly and unpredictable. MySpace, like Atari, is virtually a historical footnote now, but the company once held a dominant market share in the world of social media—until Facebook and others devised faster, more personable, more flexible and more "hip" approaches to their audience. Within a matter of months, MySpace faded from the big game in town to a has-been.

A similar market shocker has been the wholesale abandonment of those under 25 to email as a method of communication. While teens and 20-somethings may use email for matters such as college applications, they use texting on smart phones for virtually all other contacts. Even the laptop (and certainly the desktop) computer is endangered as a product by the omnipresent thumb-clicking that can be observed on smart phones in every locale, ranging from restaurants to business meeting to churches. Web designers such as Web.com are scrambling to convert last year's business—a full-screen website—to a smart phone version. Well over one million apps now exist for smart phones and a large-key, large print version of the device is under production to extend the smart phone audience to those over-40's who can't see the small print or negotiate the tiny keys like their 12-year-olds can.

The point here is that in many industry sectors disruptive technologies can include "disruptive customer choices." They are hard to predict and even more difficult include in one's analysis, given the sudden swings in preference that make market winners into market losers almost overnight. One footnote to such preferences: there is an unwritten rule, apparently, among smart phone users that a message be only a sentence or two long, and preferably just a phrase or abbreviation (OMG). This "need for speed" in messaging does not augur well for advertisers who think that eyes on the smart phone translate into patience to consider their advertisement. In the fast-paced world of texting, an ad may appear to be only an annoyance, and one that smart phone users will punish by avoiding the advertised product entirely.

```
        ┌──────────────┐
        │   INDUSTRY   │
        │   ANALYSIS   │
        └──────────────┘
          ╱          ╲
  ┌──────────┐    ┌──────────────┐
  │  PROFIT  │    │ KEY SUCCESS  │
  │ POTENTIAL│    │   FACTORS    │
  └──────────┘    └──────────────┘
```

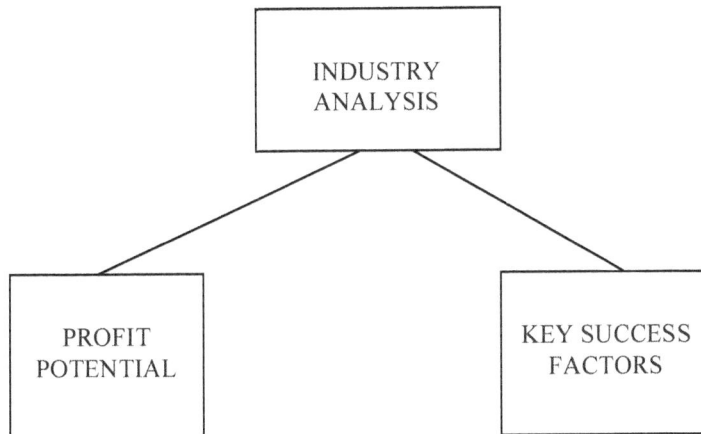

As the chart above shows, once an industry analysis is complete, it is time to proceed to competitive analysis. In fact, a good industry analysis will make the competitive analysis process far more efficient. Rather than pursuing a lengthy, unfocused competitive analysis effort, industry analysis allows the strategist to concentrate on the relationship of the competitor to the key industry segments and the key success factors.

Analysis of one's competitors should address and answer three fundamental questions. First, what level of emphasis will my competitor place on my business, *i.e.,* what level of strategic resources are they likely to devote to the business? Answering this question in turn requires an understanding of the overall financial strength of the competitor and the relative prioritization of the line of business against which you compete within the competitor's portfolio of businesses. A price cut with the goal of gaining market share will be a very effective weapon against a financially weak competitor which does not place a high emphasis on the business against which you compete. On the other hand, the exact same strategy will fail dramatically if the competitor is financially strong and if the business against which you compete is the competitor's highest priority area of investment. That competitor will match your price cut to prevent you from gaining share, and you will both wind up losing.

Secondly, a competitive analysis should tell you how your competitor will compete in your business, or, in other words, how the competitor will spend the strategic resources it has at its disposal. This analysis should focus primarily on the areas where the key success factors lie, as identified in the industry analysis. In general, however, good competitive analysis will predict how the competitor will compete in terms of three things: (a) how the competitor will come to market, *i.e.* with what product, price, sales and distribution, marketing effort, customer service, and so forth; (b) the competitor's cost position; and (c) the competitor's research & development efforts that will change its marketing or cost position over time. Product R&D may improve the competitor's future ability to market, while process R&D may improve the competitor's future cost position.

Finally, the third area of competitive analysis is an evaluation of the competitor's personality or culture. Every company has a culture, and cultures aren't easy to change. In fact, company cultures are a lot like a person's personality. If an individual is aware that his personality is lacking in some way, it still isn't easy for the individual to actually change that personality. The same is true for companies: every company tends to "like" to compete in certain ways, and just because top management or strategists decide to do otherwise, it does not necessarily mean the company will be *able* to change. A good evaluation of a company's culture will go a long way towards predicting the future actions of your competitor. (For detail on competitive analysis, see this book's other companion volume, *Understanding the Competition: A Practical Guide to Competitive Analysis*.)

Nowhere is the issue of culture more apparent than in mergers. Almost inevitably, the culture of one partner to the merger (as with Getty and Texaco) takes on an air of superiority and dominance, reducing the culture of the other partner to private humiliation and secret sabotage. Therefore, pay particular attention to the "Culture" box in the following flowchart. Companies in general do not like to budget significant funds for nurturing culture in a productive direction. But the money these companies save in not addressing culture change is, in fact, spent many times over in HR hearings, legal suits, unwanted resignations, and the decreased productivity that comes with low company morale or the perception of an "A team" and a "B team" in terms of who really matters within the firm.

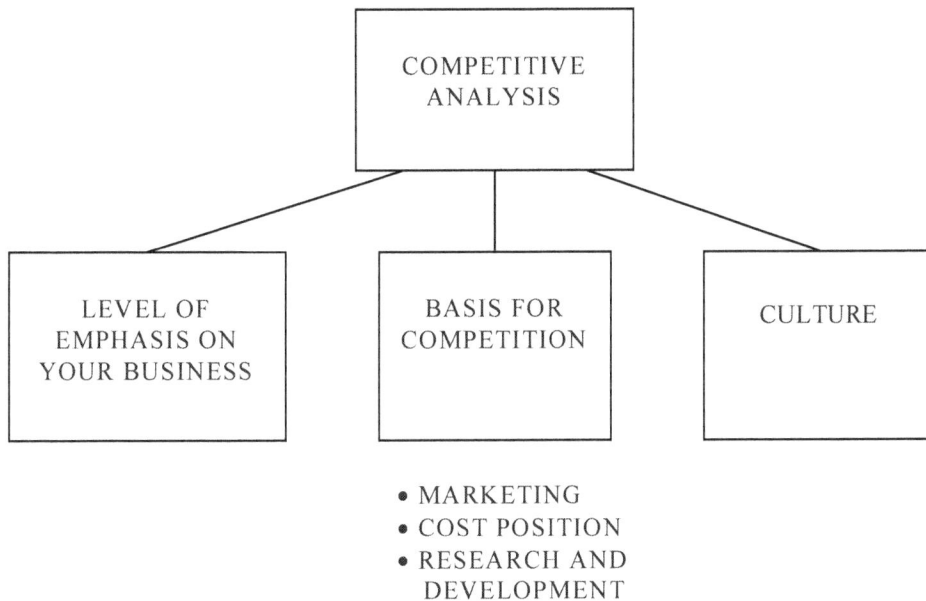

```
                    ┌─────────────────┐
                    │   COMPETITIVE   │
                    │    ANALYSIS     │
                    └─────────────────┘
              ┌────────────┼────────────┐
    ┌─────────────┐ ┌─────────────┐ ┌─────────────┐
    │  LEVEL OF   │ │  BASIS FOR  │ │   CULTURE   │
    │ EMPHASIS ON │ │ COMPETITION │ │             │
    │YOUR BUSINESS│ │             │ │             │
    └─────────────┘ └─────────────┘ └─────────────┘
```

- MARKETING
- COST POSITION
- RESEARCH AND
  DEVELOPMENT

The last step in the analysis is strategy development, or the formulation of your company's strategy. Once again, good industry analysis and competitive analysis will make the strategy development process more efficient. If one understands ·· through industry analysis ·· what it takes to succeed in the business, and if the competitive analysis identifies how the competitors stack up relative to those key success factors, the strategy development effort is vastly simplified. It becomes the process of identifying how you company can out-perform competitors relative to those key success factors.

Elements of Strategic Analysis

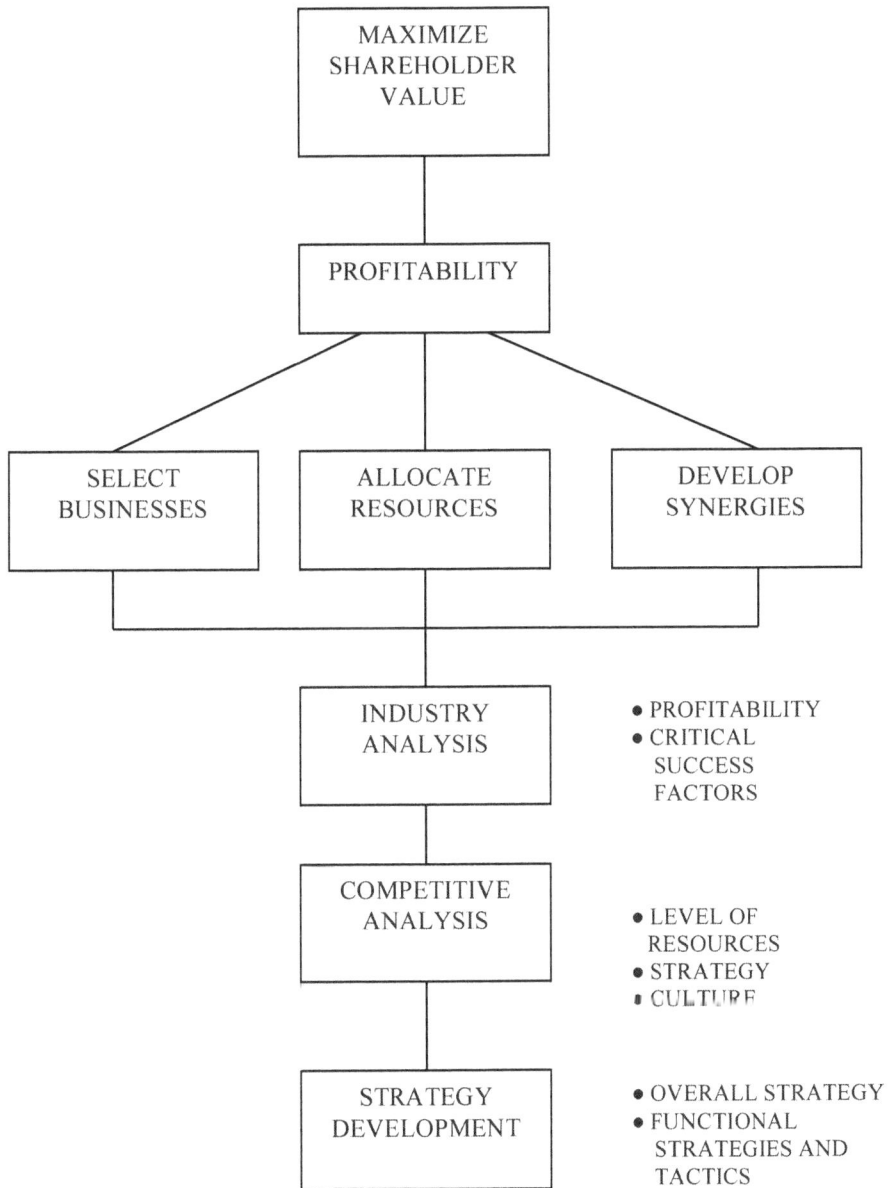

```
        ┌─────────────────┐
        │    MAXIMIZE      │
        │  SHAREHOLDER     │
        │     VALUE        │
        └────────┬────────┘
                 │
        ┌────────┴────────┐
        │  PROFITABILITY   │
        └─────────────────┘
```

| SELECT BUSINESSES | ALLOCATE RESOURCES | DEVELOP SYNERGIES |

| INDUSTRY ANALYSIS | • PROFITABILITY
• CRITICAL SUCCESS FACTORS |

| COMPETITIVE ANALYSIS | • LEVEL OF RESOURCES
• STRATEGY
• CULTURE |

| STRATEGY DEVELOPMENT | • OVERALL STRATEGY
• FUNCTIONAL STRATEGIES AND TACTICS |

Strategy development translates into a series of functional strategies: strategies for product, pricing, sales and distribution, marketing, manufacturing or operations, research & development, and so forth.

However, the major difference between good and bad strategy development processes is very basic. Less effective strategy development processes tend to develop these functional strategies in a relative vacuum. These processes include plans to build new plants, introduce new products, change prices, and so forth.

But they do not do a good job of demonstrating the relationship between those strategies and the industry and competitive analysis. They also do not demonstrate how those strategies will translate into superior profitability.

The following framework, developed by the American Productivity & Quality Center (APQC) and used here by permission, provides a helpful step-by-step path for developing strategies that link product or service quality with profitability.

APQC PROCESS CLASSIFICATION FRAMEWORK^{SM} (PCF)

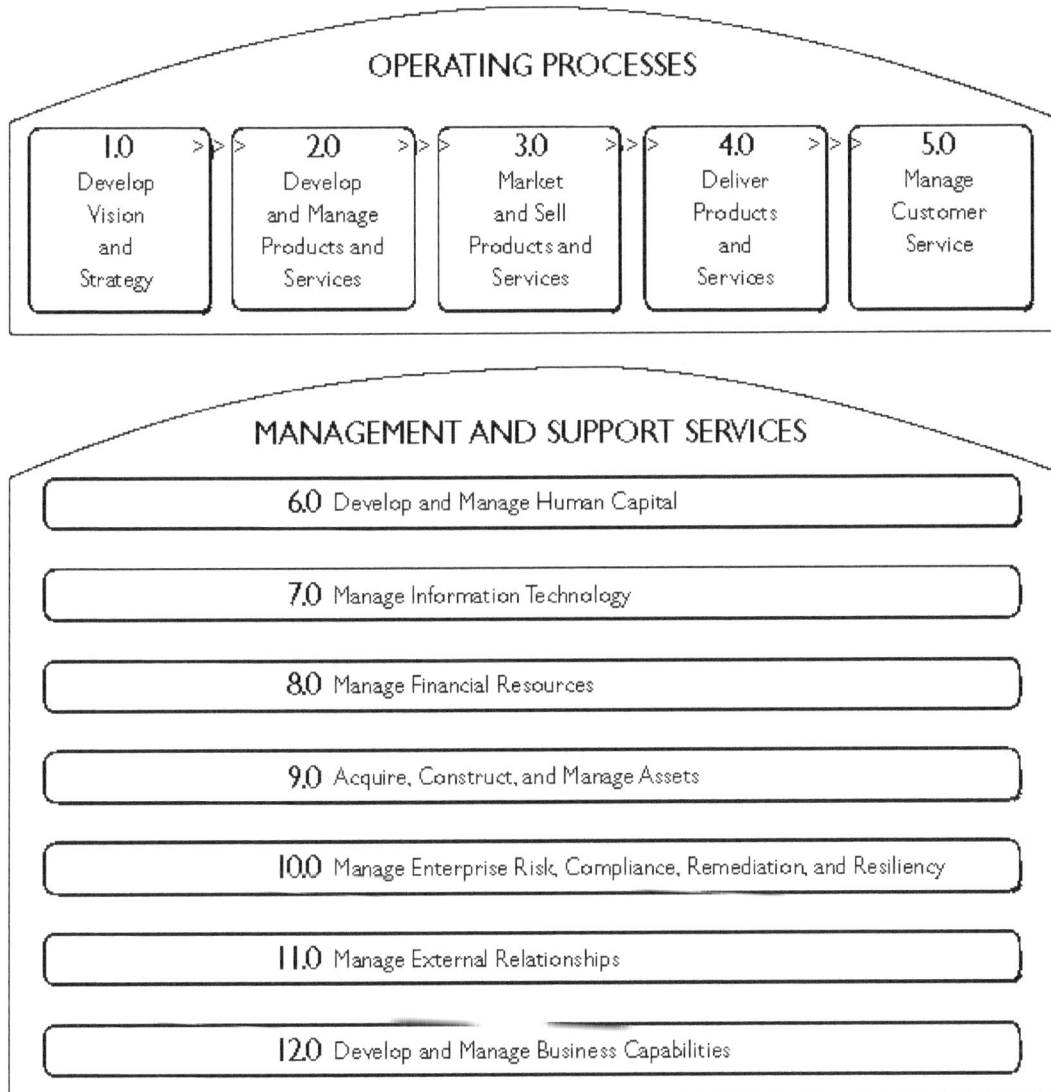

OPERATING PROCESSES

1.0 Develop Vision and Strategy	2.0 Develop and Manage Products and Services	3.0 Market and Sell Products and Services	4.0 Deliver Products and Services	5.0 Manage Customer Service

MANAGEMENT AND SUPPORT SERVICES

6.0 Develop and Manage Human Capital

7.0 Manage Information Technology

8.0 Manage Financial Resources

9.0 Acquire, Construct, and Manage Assets

10.0 Manage Enterprise Risk, Compliance, Remediation, and Resiliency

11.0 Manage External Relationships

12.0 Develop and Manage Business Capabilities

Effective strategy development, on the other hand, ties these functional strategies very closely to the conclusions of the industry and competitive analysis. In fact, until you can convince yourself that your various functional strategies will enable you to out-perform competitors relative to the key success factors, in attractive segments of the industry, you have not demonstrated how your company will earn superior profitability. Until you do so, the strategy development process is not really finished.

The Role of Benchmarking

Benchmarking is a rigorous process for tying strategy development to industry and competitive analysis. It is a method for:

1) measuring the performance of your "best-in-class" competitors relative to your industry's key success factors;

2) determining *how* the best-in-class achieve those performance levels; and

3) using that data as a basis for your own company's targets, strategies, and implementation.

A rigorous benchmarking process will ensure that the business' strategy will accomplish a competitive position that will out-perform competitors relative to the key success factors, as outlined in the following flowchart.

```
                    ┌─────────────────────────┐
                    │      BENCHMARKING       │
                    └─────────────────────────┘
```

MEASURE THE PERFORMANCE OF THE "BEST-IN-CLASS" COMPANIES	DETERMINE HOW THAT PERFORMANCE IS ACHIEVED	USE A BASIS FOR OWN COMPANY'S TARGETS / STRATEGIES / IMPLEMENTATION

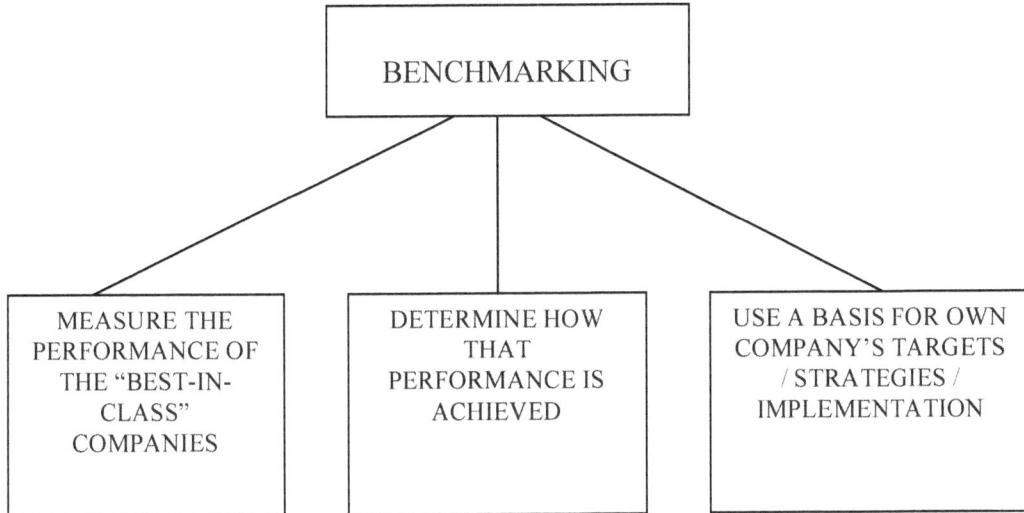

As indicated in the RIM example in Chapter 1, benchmarking can be carried out at two levels: strategic and operational. Strategic benchmarking -- the subject of Part II -- is a process for insuring that the company's fundamental strategy is consistent with the industry key success factors and that it takes into account the impact of competitors' strategies. Operational benchmarking (Part III), far more detailed, is a process for ensuring that specific aspects of a company's functional operations -- such as manufacturing cost, sales force efficiency, research and development programs, IT infrastructure, etc. -- are sufficient to out-perform competitors in those specific operational areas. A third type of benchmarking -- "Business Model" benchmarking -- is a variant on the first two and is described in Part IV.

The Evolution of Benchmarking

Benchmarking is the latest focus in the evolution of competitive analysis over the last couple of decades. Historically, many companies conducted competitive analysis on a purely intuitive basis. However, the maturing of our economy, the entry of foreign competitors, and increasingly sophisticated and price sensitive customers have led companies to realize that explicit, careful competitive analysis is necessary to win in today's world.

The first explicit competitive processes were comprised largely of competitive data-gathering. Companies began to regularly gather various pieces of information about their competitors.

Companies soon learned that this was not enough. Competitive data considered in isolation rarely yields insights about one's own strategy. The second step in the evolution consisted of competitive *analysis* or the clever interpretation of competitive data in order to predict what a competitor's future strategy is likely to be. Today, most companies have some sort of process in place to systematically analyze competitors' future strategies.

However, as the environment in many industries has gotten increasingly competitive and difficult, companies have found that good competitive analysis, while absolutely necessary, is not enough to ensure competitive advantage and strong profitability. During the last few years, a variety of companies large and small have begun to regularly conduct benchmarking analyses, to make sure that they are truly achieving competitive advantage at both the strategic and operational level, and not just predicting what competitors are going to do. Benchmarking has caught on very rapidly, and the companies that have taken the lead have already seen strong returns in terms of their competitive position and financial results.

Examples range from the largest to the smallest firms. A multi-national bank considered the metric "wait time" as an important component of its benchmarking for competitive edge. The bank recognized that wait time for the customer is an almost universally negative experience in all aspects of life, whether waiting for a vital part to be delivered to their business or a pizza to their home. Standing in long lines to make a deposit or conduct other business at a bank branch was identified as a key customer dissatisfier. On a scale of 1 to 100 (100 marking complete satisfaction), the bank calculated that a customer satisfaction score of 92 on its benchmarking instrument would constitute an achievable objective that would significantly surpass comparable scores by competitors. The bank devoted human and financial resources toward closing the gap between its existing customer score for customer satisfaction in relation to wait time and its objective of 92 percent. Once that goal had been achieved, the bank continued its benchmarking in an effort to instill continuous improvement as a cultural pillar of the firm.

At the other end of the "size" spectrum, Pal's Sudden Service, a small fast-food chain and a Baldrige Quality Award winner, found that through benchmarking they achieved best-in-class performance for drive-thru and overall restaurant operations when measured not only against similar sized firms but also against the fast-food giants. Pal's became so convinced of the value of benchmarking that it opened an educational institute to train other organizations. Many fast food firms now benchmark against Pal's practices as best-in-class aspirations for their own companies.

As the Internet and mobile worlds have grown so has the opportunity to tap into the consumer using social tools like Twitter and Facebook, or internet activity as new ways to benchmark. These tools allow new ways of tracking and benchmarking key indicators of success like image and customer satisfaction. The internet has also allowed companies to benchmark the B2B interface, not just B2C interactions. Multiple vendors offer ways of tracking B2B activity using search tools like Google Alerts to record the press and media coverage of specific markets, companies and products or services, allowing for near automated benchmarking of these activities and instant reporting through Internet portals. Indian companies have been very successful in building and customized these types of tools. Reliance Industries Ltd. (RIL), Oil and Natural Gas Corporation (ONGC), Infosys, and Sun Pharma are at the top of the list of progressive Indian firms tracking B2B activity through a plethora of Internet "windows" into the attitudes and business choices of their customers.

Another type of benchmarking that has been growing in recent years is cross-industry, or out-of-industry benchmarking. Of course, it takes an imaginative mind to forecast which cross industry or out-of-industry companies might pertain to your benchmarking. This is where executive encouragement to "think outside the box" can be extremely valuable. In making the momentous decision to drop "Pizza" from its company name and store signage, Domino's had to think outside their usual world of pizza production and entertain the thought that they could become the predominant urban food provider, especially for large and mid-sized cities. This paradigm shift in their thinking involved them in a world they didn't know well—everything having to do with food delivery from the local Chinese restaurant to the plethora of bike- and car-based food delivery services already in existence. Domino's had to weigh whether they could make a profit amidst this disorganized, low-paying band of food deliverers. With the growth of benchmarking as a standard tool offered by consultants around the world, today companies can quickly identify their low hanging inefficiencies within their own industries. As a result, they have been increasingly looking for other ideas to better compete against their leading competitors and, in so doing, have been increasingly looking for related examples in totally different industries. We will talk about this more in the next chapter.

Chapter 3

A Seven-step Process for Benchmarking

Benchmarking is an analytical process for rigorously measuring your company's operations versus the "best-in-class" companies both in and outside of your industry. Insights generated by the benchmarking process allow you to identify and implement specific actions needed to close the gap between your company and the best-in-class.

A successful benchmarking analysis includes seven steps:

1) Determining which functional areas within your operation are to be benchmarked, *i.e.* those that will benefit most from the benchmarking process;

2) Identifying the key factors and variables with which to measure those functions;

3) Selecting the best-in-class companies for each item to be benchmarked ·· those companies that perform each function at the lowest cost, with the highest degree of customer satisfaction, etc.

Best-in-class companies can be your direct competitors (domestic or foreign) or even companies from a different industry. For instance, any company seeking to improve the effectiveness of its customer service technicians might gain from analyzing how IBM achieves its superior service rating;

4)   Measuring the performance of the best-in-class companies for each benchmark variable;

5)   Measuring your own performance for each variable and determining the gap between you and the best-in-class. This involves researching how other companies have improved the functional areas you are benchmarking through online secondary research of case studies and primary research on specific best-in-class companies;

6)   Specifying programs and actions to meet and surpass the competition;

7)   Implementing these programs by setting specific improvement targets and deadlines, and by developing a monitoring process to review and update the analysis over time. There is obvious danger, needless to say, in blind imitation of best-in-class companies. This "me-too" syndrome follows the logic that "if it worked for them, it will work for us." But such thinking defies the wisdom that successful firms differentiate themselves in terms of their value proposition for the customer. Probably the best advice is to borrow specific aspects of best-in-class companies that you can make uniquely your own, primarily by blending an outside "best practice" with your company culture and, from the beginning, labeling the item borrowed in some new way that accords with your company image.

The Benchmarking Process

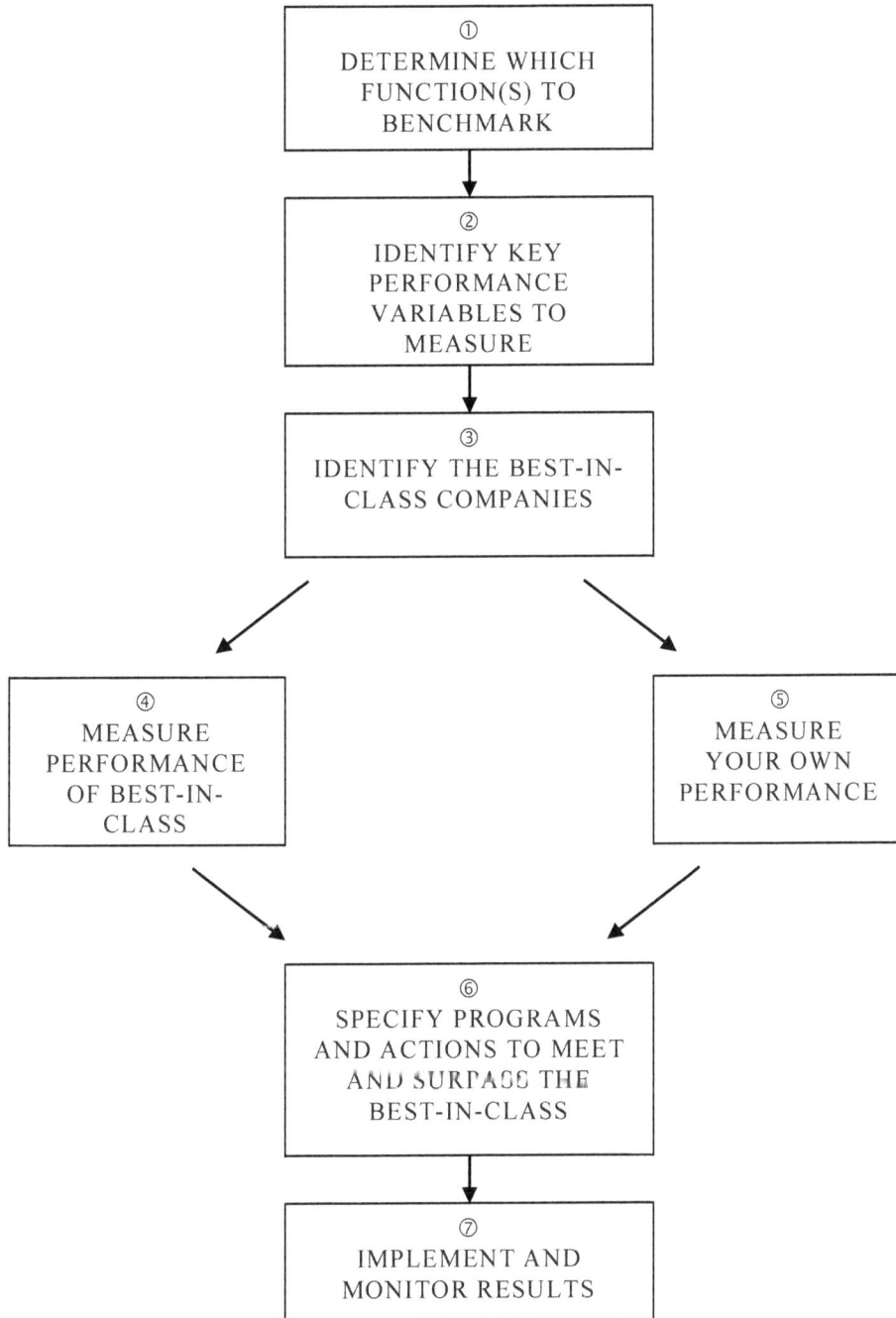

```
┌─────────────────────────┐
│            ①            │
│   DETERMINE WHICH       │
│   FUNCTION(S) TO        │
│   BENCHMARK             │
└─────────────────────────┘
            │
            ▼
┌─────────────────────────┐
│            ②            │
│   IDENTIFY KEY          │
│   PERFORMANCE           │
│   VARIABLES TO          │
│   MEASURE               │
└─────────────────────────┘
            │
            ▼
┌─────────────────────────┐
│            ③            │
│   IDENTIFY THE BEST-IN- │
│   CLASS COMPANIES       │
└─────────────────────────┘
      ↙             ↘
┌──────────────┐   ┌──────────────┐
│      ④       │   │      ⑤       │
│  MEASURE     │   │  MEASURE     │
│  PERFORMANCE │   │  YOUR OWN    │
│  OF BEST-IN- │   │  PERFORMANCE │
│  CLASS       │   │              │
└──────────────┘   └──────────────┘
      ↘             ↙
┌─────────────────────────┐
│            ⑥            │
│   SPECIFY PROGRAMS      │
│   AND ACTIONS TO MEET   │
│   AND SURPASS THE       │
│   BEST-IN-CLASS         │
└─────────────────────────┘
            │
            ▼
┌─────────────────────────┐
│            ⑦            │
│   IMPLEMENT AND         │
│   MONITOR RESULTS       │
└─────────────────────────┘
```

None of the steps listed above is completely new or "revolutionary." However, experience has shown that businesses which explicitly focus on benchmarking analysis are likely to achieve significantly greater improvement than companies which merely count on steps one through seven to happen by themselves.

Step 1: Determining Which Functions to Benchmark

One of the surest ways for a benchmarking process to fail is to try to benchmark everything at once. Benchmarking analysis requires time, effort, and management attention. This means that the various functions within a company must be prioritized: you must decide which functions should be benchmarked first, second, and so forth, and which should not be benchmarked at all.

There are no set rules as to which function should be benchmarked first, but there are four key criteria which should be applied within your organization in determining your priorities:

• *Which functions represent the highest percentage of cost?* If your engineering function is found to be 20% higher cost than the competition, and if engineering represents a large portion of your cost (say, 40% of your total cost), then the potential reduction is 20% x 40%, or 8% of your total cost, which, in turn, will have an enormous impact on your margin. On the other hand, that same 20% savings on engineering cost, if applied to an engineering function which represents only 2% of cost, will have an impact of only 20% x 2%, or 0.4% of total cost. Obviously, by focusing on those steps that represent the greatest portion of cost, you are likely to identify the potential cost savings that have the greatest impact on your overall organization.

• *Which functions play the greatest role in differentiating competitors in the marketplace?* Some functions may represent a small portion of cost, but may be absolutely crucial in determining who wins and loses in the fight to win customers. Functions like advertising, research and development, sales, and specific portions of the manufacturing process may have competitive importance way out of proportion to their percentage of total cost. Such functions represent high priorities for benchmarking, since a gain in competitive position in those functions can have a major impact on the business.

You should think of prioritizing functions through the lens of the 80%-20% rule where the metric is delivering competitive advantage. Some of your organization's functions may be very expensive like manufacturing, much of which may be essential to be in the market, but not necessarily drive competitive advantage and so of lesser importance than other far cheaper functions. An example is self-injectable drugs where the manufacturing of the drug is complex and expensive, but the final device that the drug is put into for the patient to self-inject is very important competitively. A good design that is very easy to use will gain mark share over one that is complex and difficult for the patient. As a result, drug companies spend a lot of time and effort designing the right delivery device, while run low cost manufacturing operations and the final cost of the delivery device to the patient is significantly less than 10% the cost of the drug.

- *Which functions have the greatest room for improvement?* Even though you may be beginning a formal benchmarking process for the first time, you and your company have considerable experience analyzing your operations. You probably already have an intuitive sense as to which functions are top notch and which functions are not up to snuff. Those functions which you intuitively feel have greatest room for improvement represent higher benchmark priorities.

- *Which functions are capable of improvement?* Because of politics, regulation, organizational constraints, or other factors, some functions may yield more easily to improvement than others. If your company is high cost in a function, but in reality there's very little your company can do about it, then that function is not a priority for benchmarking.

None of these four criteria should be taken as an absolute. Instead, each should be considered and applied to each function in your organization. Those functions for which the answers to these questions are in general most positive should be the functions that are benchmarked first. The key point to remember is that benchmarking is not an end in itself, but a means to an end. The criteria are designed so as to select functions where you are likely to find potential improvements that are both important and achievable. There is nothing to be gained from benchmarking functions where the likely improvements are either very small or not very achievable.

Using these criteria, the functions that companies have benchmarked include manufacturing and various sub-segments of manufacturing (components manufacturing, sub-assembly, assembly, etc.), marketing, sales, distribution, research and development, engineering, human resources, data processing, purchasing, administration, finance, strategic planning, operations, IT infrastructure, and numerous others. Most companies start with anywhere from one to three or four functions, and then proceed to the lower priority functions over time.

Step 2: Selecting the Key Performance Variables

Benchmarking analysis measures a function in terms of specific variables of operations and performance -- such as the number of accounts covered per salesperson, labor productivity, raw material yield in the manufacturing process, cycle time in the engineering process, etc. The specific variables to be benchmarked vary widely across different benchmarking analyses. However, the items to be benchmarked usually fall into several broad categories.

For *operational benchmarking* efforts, two broad categories of performance variables may be benchmarked. They are:

- *Internal benchmarks*, such as cost variables, like labor efficiency, compensation levels, overhead costs, etc.; These can also include "resource utilization" variables such as training days per year, or number of FTEs in specific functions, like sales forces, and metrics used to manage them such as customer calls per day, or wait time for in-house customer call centers. Internal benchmarks are succinctly categorized by the APQC as follows:

APQC PCF^{SM} – 4.0 DELIVERY PRODUCTS AND SERVICES

4.1	Plan for and align supply chain resources
4.2	Procure materials and services
4.3	Produce/Manufacture/Deliver product
4.4	Deliver service to customer
4.5	Manage logistics and warehousing

APQC PCF^{SM} – 5.0 MANAGE CUSTOMER SEVICE

5.1	Develop customer care/customer service strategy
5.2	Plan and manage customer service operations
5.3	Measure and evaluate customer service operations

APQC PCF^{SM} – 6.0 DEVELOP AND MANAGE HUMAN CAPITAL

6.1	Develop and manage human resources (HR) planning, policies, and strategies
6.2	Recruit, source, and select employees
6.3	Develop and counsel employees
6.4	Manage employee relations
6.5	Reward and retain employees
6.6	Redeploy and retire employees
6.7	Manage employee information and analytics
6.8	Manage employee communication

APQC PCF^{SM} – 7.0 MANAGE INFORMATION TECHNOLOGY

7.1	Manage the business of information technology
7.2	Develop and manage IT customer relationships
7.3	Develop and implement security, privacy, and data protection controls
7.4	Manage enterprise information
7.5	Develop and maintain information technology solutions
7.6	Deploy information technology solutions
7.7	Deliver and support information technology services

APQC PCF^{SM} – 8.0 MANAGE FINANCIAL RESOURCES

8.1	Perform planning and management accounting
8.2	Perform revenue accounting
8.3	Perform general accounting and reporting
8.4	Manage fixed asset project accounting
8.5	Process payroll
8.6	Process accounts payable and expense reimbursements
8.7	Manage treasury operations
8.8	Manage internal controls

8.9	Manage taxes
8.10	Manage international funds/consolidation
8.11	Perform global trade services

• *External benchmarks,* or "differentiation" variables, *i.e.,* variables that measure the degree of customer satisfaction with your offering in the external marketplace.

Differentiation variables include such factors as product line breadth and feature sets available, product quality, service levels and service quality, image, and overall customer satisfaction. The APQC delineates differentiation variable in the following tables:

APQC PCF^{SM} – 1.0 DEVELOP AND MANAGE PRODUCTS AND SERVICES

1.1	Define the business concept and long-term vision
1.2	Develop business strategy
1.3	Manage strategic initiatives

APQC PCF^{SM} – 2.0 DEVELOP VISION AND STRATEGY

2.1	Manage product and service portfolio
2.2	Develop products and services

APQC PCF^{SM} – 3.0 MARKET AND SELL PRODUCTS AND SERVICES

3.1	Understand markets, customers and capabilities
3.2	Develop marketing strategy
3.3	Develop sales strategy
3.4	Develop and manage marketing plans
3.5	Develop and manage sales plans

APQC PCF^{SM} – 9.0 ACQUIRE, CONSTRUCT AND MANAGE ASSETS

9.1	Design and construct/acquire nonproductive assets
9.2	Plan maintenance work
9.3	Obtain and install assets, equipment, and tools (
9.4	Dispose of productive and nonproductive assets

APQC PCF^{SM} – 10.0 MANAGE ENTERPRISE RISK, COMPLIANCE, REMEDIATION AND RESILIANCY

10.1	Manage enterprise risk
10.2	Manage compliance
10.3	Manage remediation efforts
10.4	Manage business resiliency

APQC PCF^{SM} – 11.0 MANAGE EXTERNAL RELATIONSHIPS

11.1	Build investor relationships
11.2	Manage government and industry relationships
11.3	Manage relations with board of directors
11.4	Manage legal and ethical issues

Strategic benchmarking usually involves measurement of the best-in-class companies in terms of the following:

- Financial performance, including market share, sales growth, profitability as measured in a number of different ways, and so forth;

- Company strategy, including overall strategy and strategy for each of the various functional areas. By correlating the different strategies with financial performance, the strategic benchmarking effort identifies those strategies which are the most successful in achieving the desired financial results.

In Parts II and III, we will outline in much greater detail specific performance variables to be used in both strategic benchmarking and operational benchmarking efforts. Appendices A (Ford's Taurus and Sable, Appendix B (Benchmarking at Xerox), and Appendix C (Decisions about Internal Customer Call Centers) provides case details of how these variables have been applied to the benefit of the companies involved.

Step 3: Identifying the Best-In-Class Companies

The goal of any benchmarking analysis is to identify companies which are superior performers, so that their superior performance levels can be used as targets for your own company's operations.

The so-called "best-in-class" companies may be selected from four different categories:

- Direct competitors: For example, Ford has benchmarked itself against Honda, BMW, General Motors, Chrysler, and dozens of other direct competitors.

- Parallel competitors: This category includes companies that are basically in the same business as your company, but that do not compete with your company directly. For example, a bank in North Carolina might successfully benchmark various aspects of its operation against banks in other parts of the country. By looking beyond your direct competitors, you are more likely to uncover creative approaches which enable you to leapfrog your competition.

- Latent competitors: In some cases, this can be the most important category of all. Latent competitors are companies with which you do not yet compete, but which loom as threats in the future. For decades, the auto companies in Detroit effectively benchmarked their operations against each other. Ford watched General Motors and Chrysler, General Motors watched Ford and Chrysler, and so forth. Only when the Japanese and the North Europeans had succeeded in taking large amounts of market share did the American companies start benchmarking themselves against those competitors in a serious way. Japanese auto manufacturers, like Honda and Toyota, prided themselves of reliability, North European automakers, like Volvo, on safety and Germans, like BMW and Mercedes, on engineering. Detroit companies on the other hand looked for built in obsolescence and exterior looks. In retrospect, it is obvious that the Americans should have benchmarked themselves against foreign competitors long before those companies came to American shores. If they had done so and cross-checked with the views of the customer, they might have understood the looming competitive threat, or at least limited their market share loss as the Japanese and Europeans attacked the U.S. market. Today, Detroit is keenly aware of foreign competition which has expanded to include South Korea, India and, most likely in the near future, China.

When latent competitors enter the market, they often re-define the accepted levels of performance by either lowering costs or offering a higher quality product or service. For precisely that reason, benchmarking against latent competitors *before* they compete with you can be the most valuable form of benchmarking in some instances. This applies especially to competitors who have relatively low barriers of entry, such as the tsunami of Uber operations that sprang up, seemingly overnight, only to be challenged (so far unsuccessfully) by competing services such as Lyft. The same point can be made of airbnb.com, whose main obstacle to profitability seems to be the fight they are encountering with local housing and zoning ordinances, not to mention the pressure brought on city officials from local "mom-and-pop" hotels whose businesses are dramatically impacted by the entry of airbnb.com into their marketplace.

- Out-of-industry companies: A particularly creative type of benchmarking involves measuring your performance against companies in completely different industries. As we have already mentioned, this type of benchmarking has been growing in importance in recent. For example, when Hewlett Packard (HP) wanted to improve its supply chain and cut down time between product design and shipping to the trade, it looked to the fashion design company Benetton. The problem in the fast moving fashion industry is that it is not clear until well into any season which would be the best selling colors. So rather than pre-dying the wood and then knit sweaters, Benetton knits its sweaters in plain wool and dyes them afterwards when it has good market feedback on the likely winning colors for each season. By making this major changes in its supply chain, Benetton gained major competitive advantage as it significantly increased its success in bringing the color to the market compared to its competitors. By studying Benetton, HP redesigned its printer manufacturing and supply chain along the same lines, so it could assembly the best printer for the market at the last moment as consumer and business demands shifted, rather than the traditional process of predefining a design and building well before it was offered to the market.

Benchmarking against out-of-industry competitors can be a key way to leapfrog your existing competition. If you are trying to improve your operations only by measuring what competitors are doing, you are constantly in a catch-up mode. If you can bring in new techniques and processes from outside the industry, you have the opportunity to get ahead of your competition.

Once you have generated a list of potential companies against which to benchmark, how do you narrow the list down and decide exactly which companies to use? Again, there are no hard and fast rules, and each of the following guidelines have exceptions. Nonetheless, the guidelines which follow apply to most situations and should be used as a starting point:

- In general, you should limit your list of benchmark companies to between four and six companies. In some cases, eight or ten companies are necessary, and in some cases two to three will suffice. In general, however, less than four does not provide enough variety and good data, and more than six produces diminishing returns. Companies that benchmark against ten competitors often find they learn little from the seventh through tenth competitor that they didn't learn from the first six, particularly if the first six were chosen carefully.

• Try to use as diverse a set of companies as reasonably possible. For example, if you have half-a-dozen low cost Far Eastern competitors and half-a-dozen specialty competitors in the United States, use some of each. The reason for this is again that benchmarking is a means to an end, not an end in itself. If you choose six similar competitors, the data on the last few of them will be "nice to know," but will tell you little about your own operations that you didn't learn from the first three competitors that you studied. The more diverse the set of competitors, the more insights you're likely to generate for your own operations.

• Try in general to pick companies with the best bottom line performance, *i.e.*, the best market share, sales growth, profitability, or whatever. In general, the companies doing best are the ones that you're going to learn the most from, and there's less to learn from the marketplace losers. In particular, if there are one or two competitors in your market that really stand out as being the most successful, they definitely should be included in your benchmarking effort.

• One note of caution: do not consider benchmarking a "one and done" experience for your company. Benchmarking at its best is constant activity of a successful company, just as is adaptation in marketing and quality control. Benchmarking must be continuous precisely because the world outside your company is constantly changing.

• Finally, also pick any companies that have a particularly creative or effective strategy in the specific functional area you are benchmarking. If you're benchmarking a distribution function, for example, you may be aware of a competitor that, despite mediocre overall results, has come up with a superior way to approach distribution. By including these creative and "different" companies in your search, you again are likely to uncover the greatest amount of insight about how to improve your own operations.

Step 4: Measuring the Performance of the Best-In-Class Companies

Once you have decided which functions to benchmark, which performance variables to measure those functions by, and which companies to benchmark against, it is time to go out and gather the data for the best-in-class companies.

Data for benchmarking analyses usually comes from three types of sources: published sources, data sharing, and interviews. APQC is an invaluable source of data, http://www.apqc.org/. Its knowledgebase covers:

- BUSINESS EXCELLENCE

- FINANCIAL MANAGEMENT

- HUMAN CAPITAL MANAGEMENT

- KNOWLEDGE MANAGEMENT

- SUPPLY CHAIN MANAGEMENT

Published Sources

Published sources are the best place to start a benchmarking effort. However, rarely can all the information needed be found in published sources alone. There are several different categories of published sources of information, and their relative strengths and weaknesses are outlined below.

- *APQC*, briefly introduced in Chapter 2, is a member-based nonprofit and one of the world's leading proponents of business benchmarking, best practices, and knowledge management research. Their mission is to help organizations around the world improve productivity and quality by discovering effective methods of improvement, broadly disseminating findings, and connect individuals with one another and with the knowledge they need to improve. APQC has open standards benchmark platform where companies can submit operational and business metrics to compare against the industry and identify the gaps. APQC platform can be found at apqc.org.

- *Securities and Exchange Commission Filings* must be submitted by all public companies. These include yearly 10K's, quarterly 10Q's, and special reports such as a Prospectus or Proxy, which are filed when companies issue new securities or become involved in mergers and acquisitions. These sources provide both financial and qualitative information on companies and are typically more useful in strategic benchmarking. However, a careful combing of the filings of small and medium-sized companies can provide useful data for operational benchmarking as well.

- *Company Published Documents* include annual reports, product brochures, periodic news releases, recruiting brochures and other documents. While much of this information is general, more often than not, there will be a few "gems" of key data buried in these documents. This type of information can be collected by contacting the investor relations and/or sales offices of the benchmark company.

- *General Business and Trade Articles* are valuable information sources in many benchmarking projects. General business magazines (e.g., Business Week, Fortune) and trade magazines (e.g., Chemical Week, Advertising Age) can provide data and insights beyond that available in other sources. Most published articles are indexed in a variety of published and on-line directories.

- *Local Newspaper Articles* are the most often overlooked source of competitive benchmarking information. Many successful benchmarking efforts obtain data from local newspapers located near a competitor's headquarters, plant, or major office. These articles often contain information on hirings, layoffs, wages, key personnel changes, new products, business strategies, and so forth. In one manufacturing benchmarking analysis, a local library's files contained 20 years of articles on a particular plant and allowed the analyst to develop a detailed history of plant expansions and modifications. Some companies monitor local newspapers regularly, not only for articles, but also to review competitors' want-ad placements.

- *Analyst Reports* are documents produced by the Wall Street investment houses (e.g., Merrill Lynch, Goldman Sachs) as they evaluate investment opportunities for their clients. In general, all public companies are followed by at least one Wall Street analyst and, in most cases, by several.

Analyst reports include both financial and strategic information. To accommodate the analysts, companies often release detailed data through these documents. Analyst reports are available directly from the brokerage house or from various on-line databases.

One particularly interesting development since 2015 is the evaluation of competitive processes in terms of so-called "k"-units, an outcome of Fifth Wave Accounting practices. A k-unit is the minimal unit of change in a competitor's process of taking raw material through to finished product. Each k-unit, of course, can be monetized, with all k-units adding up to the eventual production expense of the product involved. An analysis of k-units can be useful in determining where you can achieve efficiencies in similar production by, perhaps, omitting redundant k-unit changes or combining those that are most similar. A brief example may make this concept clearer. A piece of redwood enters a factory. It will eventually exit the factory as entry-door threshold. On its way through preparation, milling, sanding, sizing, and so forth, it undergoes a specific number of k-unit changes, each of which a) cost the company money; and b) add value to the product being produced. An examination of those k-units can put you in an advantageous position to decide how your company processes can exceed those of your competitor in quality and cost. In short, you k-units have to be either fewer in number or cost less than your competitor's.

•   *Credit Reports*, available from companies like Dun & Bradstreet, are sources for information on private companies. These reports provide both financial and management data, and while they are not the best source for detailed benchmarking information, they can provide some critical pieces of data.

•   *Multi-Client Market Reports* typically focus on a particular market and its major competitors. These reports rarely provide the detailed data needed for operational cost benchmarking, but they often provide the basic market share and product information needed for strategic benchmarking.

•   *Trade Associations* often provide competitors within an industry with surveys of overall industry trends and industry average cost and performance benchmarks. In addition, within these associations, there are often particular individuals with a specific area of expertise; if they don't have the information you need, they will often refer you to someone who does. These associations are all indexed in the Encyclopedia of Associations.

• *Government Agencies* responsible for regulating industries generate a diverse array of published documents. For example, most manufacturing companies must file plant information with either the Environmental Protection Agency (EPA) or the Occupational Safety and Health Administration (OSHA). Information on the number of employees, the types of machines used, and major raw materials can often be gleaned from these filings. In the telecommunications industry, competitors must file all sorts of information with local and federal regulators, while the Pentagon is an excellent source for information on defense contractors. It often takes creativity and persistence to identify the appropriate government agencies and individuals that have this data, but the payoff can be significant.

• In addition to these excellent sources of information, one must also consider certain intangibles in assessing best-in-class competitors. What, for example, is their trend line when it comes to customer reputation? Are they on their way up or out? Is their reputation segmented in some way meaningful to your analysis—say, by age group or by ethnicity? Especially in the case of a family business, do they have a transition plan in place that augurs a prosperous future for the company, or are they living out the last days of the company founder, with no particular vision for the future? These questions are not easily answered, but without at least focus group and survey inquiry into such matters no analysis of best-in-class companies can be said to be reliable and complete.

In sum, there is an abundance of published information that should be tapped when performing a benchmarking analysis, such as APQC at www.apqc.org. While published sources are typically more valuable in strategic benchmarking, they also are the starting point for operational benchmarking. Successful benchmarking requires a complete review of all sources of published data.

Data Sharing

Some firms have very successfully shared data with other companies in order to enhance their benchmarking efforts. Various types of data sharing are legal and others are not; it is crucial that you consult your corporate attorney if you have any doubt as to whether what you are doing is appropriate. However, some types of data sharing (e.g., with out-of-industry companies) are clearly legal. Other types of data sharing go on all the time, with some corporations considering them proper and legal, and other corporations thinking otherwise. Your own company rules and the advice of your corporate attorney should be your guideline. Types of data sharing include:

- *Professional conferences*, where industry players get together to share ideas on the latest state-of-the-art techniques in the industry;

- *Direct information sharing* with out-of-industry companies. For example, in benchmarking a function such as data processing or engineering, it is quite common to find that superior companies in other industries are willing to share their successes and approaches with you in return for learning some of your state-of-the-art techniques. As these companies don't compete with you directly, you may find that you can get excellent insights and data from them without jeopardizing your own competitive position;

- *Informal sharing.* In many companies, the managers of your manufacturing plant have been to competitors' plants; your sales people come across competitors' sales people all the time; and your engineers know the engineers at your competitors. Often there is a wealth of information shared informally through these channels. What is appropriate to know and use and what isn't must be approached cautiously, and once again the guidance of your internal counsel should set the standards. However, the reality is that most companies regularly use such information, many of them considering it appropriate to do so.

External Interviews

Depending upon the level of detail of data you are seeking, published sources and information sharing will get you anywhere from 30% to 100% of what you need. When they are not sufficient, there is a wealth of external sources that can be interviewed to fill the gap. These sources include: customers, distributors, suppliers, industry experts, regulators and government officials, and the benchmark companies themselves. Different companies have different guidelines about the appropriateness of contacting competitors themselves as part of the benchmarking effort. Some companies have absolute prohibitions against talking to competitors. Others prohibit employees from doing so, but allow the hiring of third parties to contact competitors. Still other companies allow the contact but limit the types of questions that may be asked. In this area, it is absolutely essential that you consult with your company's guidelines and your corporate attorney to determine what is considered appropriate in your organization. Again, the reality is that the vast majority of companies do this sort of interviewing, often through third parties, as part of their competitive and benchmarking analysis.

Caution must be exercised in taking external information as "gospel." Clients who have had a bad experience with your competitor are likely to exaggerate the occurrence. Suppliers who have been snubbed by your competitor in some way may extend that annoyance to broad judgements about the competitor's financial stability. In other words, external comments always come with "baggage attached," and it is your job in benchmarking to discover and take into consideration the weight of that baggage.

EXAMPLE QUESTIONS FROM THE APQC INTERVIEW GUIDE

Question 1	How does your organization educate potential and active customers about benefits and services offered?
Question 2	Who is involved in the delivery of the customer education activities described in Question 1, and what are their various responsibilities?
Question 3	Describe the organizational structure surrounding customer education activities.
Question 4	Describe the resources allocated to support the customer education activities you have described so far.
Question 5	What benefits have your organization seen from customer education activities? How are these benefits measured?
Question 6	Describe the process associated with developing customer education content.
Question 7	Describe the most significant management practice that has contributed to the success of customer education operations at your organization.

The good news is that regardless of the prohibitions that apply in your organization, there are almost always enough outside sources to contact which, coupled with published sources and information sharing, yield the data necessary for benchmarking analysis. This does not mean that you can always get every piece of data that you want on every competitor. However, you can always get enough information to put together an analysis which tells you where, how, and how much your organization needs to improve.

Step 5: Measuring Your Own Performance

How to measure your own performance and compare it to that of the best-in-class companies will be discussed in detail in the sections on strategic benchmarking and operational benchmarking. However, one key issue is worth highlighting here.

Most companies conducting benchmarking analyses are able to get data on their own organizations and are able to get a large amount of good data on best-in-class companies. The problem usually is that these two sets of data are not consistent. For example, if it is cost data, it may be based on different accounting systems or spread over different organizational entities.

The trickiest and most crucial part of the benchmarking process is to get the internal data and the external data on an "apples-to-apples" basis. In fact, organizations doing benchmarking for the first time often misunderstand the most important part of the process: instead they focus on the difficulty of getting outside data. However, the reason they are having that difficulty is because they think they have to get the outside data in exactly the same form as their internal data, which is often impossible. The companies that do benchmarking well get outside data and inside data in different forms, but develop creative ways to translate the two into a common ground for comparison. In particular, there are some clever but relatively simple ways to take disparate cost information and still produce "apples-to-apples" comparisons of internal costs and best-in-class company costs. These methodologies will be discussed in detail later in this book.

There is one other factor to keep in mind when gathering data on internal operations and external competitors. Benchmarking -- and competitive analysis in general -- is a field in which the ability and willingness to estimate are crucial. It is an area where directional accuracy, not accounting accuracy, is the goal. In other words, the goal is not to get information precise to the third decimal place, but to get information precise enough to identify areas where improvement is needed and to identify how that improvement can be achieved. If you are not sure whether further accuracy is needed in gathering a certain piece of data, ask yourself this question: "If I had another level of accuracy, would I do anything different based on it, or does the level of accuracy I have already tell me enough to know what to do?" Often you'll find that the final level of accuracy which could be pursued would provide you with relatively little additional information about what you need to do. For example, good cost benchmarking analyses usually identify areas where you are high cost by 5 or 10 or 20%. Knowing whether you are high cost by 5.2% or 5.8% has little bearing on what future actions your organization should take.

Step 6: Specify Programs and Actions to Close the Gap

The programs and action steps that come out of successful benchmarking analyses usually fall into four categories:

- *"Try harder":* In this category, the company identifies that it is high cost, has a poor quality sales force, or whatever, and concludes that it just must buckle down and try harder to close the gap. While trying harder is a good thing, one should be skeptical of a plan that includes only this step. Usually your organization is already trying pretty hard, and unless there is a fundamental change in systems, people, strategy, or something else, you won't accomplish your objectives merely by telling everyone to try harder than they're trying already.

• *Emulate the competition*: Some of the actions recommended by benchmarking analysis are based on emulating the successful actions of the competition. While this is often the best you can do, if an entire strategy is based purely on emulation, it usually has little chance of success. If all you're doing is copying the things that other competitors are doing, you have little chance to get ahead, especially since they'll probably be moving ahead while you're catching up.

• *Leapfrog the competition*: A successful strategy based on a benchmarking analysis should include some functional elements that actually leapfrog or get ahead of the competition. You are most likely to find these by studying companies outside the industry or companies in other segments of the market that may be further ahead in certain functional areas than your existing competitors. An example of such leap-frogging was the decision in Uganda to support cell-phone companies at the same time that surrounding companies were stringing telephone lines and scrounging for second-hand dial-up telephones from Europe and the U.K. The decision proved prudent: in a matter of weeks, Ugandans had access to telephone services around the world while their neighbors were still trying to figure out the area codes for the rest of their country.

• *Change the rules:* Sometimes, a realistic benchmarking assessment concludes that there is no way that you can catch up or get ahead of the competition given the current rules of the game in your industry. For example, if labor cost is the whole key to success, and your average cost of labor is $35/hour while you're competing against Chinese competitors with an average labor cost of $2/hour, no realistic strategy is going to close that gap unless you are willing to become a Korean competitor yourself. However, companies that have been faced with this situation have often used the benchmarking process to come up with a strategy to change the basis for success. Thus they avoid gaps that just cannot be closed. For example, one competitor that manufactured a wide range of components sold to OEMs found that they were higher cost than the Far Eastern competition and lower quality in terms of engineering know-how than the European competition. They were boxed in from both sides. However, they successfully designed a strategy, patterned after benchmark companies from outside their industry that enabled them to connect their various component products into a unique system which offered a variety of advantages to the OEMs. By changing the rules of the game, they carved out a successful niche for themselves in the marketplace and have enjoyed superior financial results ever since.

Obviously, any benchmarking analysis that does not translate into programs and actions that are implemented successfully has not been worthwhile. All of the following are needed in order for successful implementation to take place:

- *Translation of the analysis into recommendations*: Some benchmarking analyses have failed because the analysts saw it as an interesting exercise to gather some good comparison data, yet failed to complete the process by developing recommendations to close gaps between the best-in-class and their own companies. All too often analysts do not find a "champion" prior to starting their work, as a result they do not have anyone to take action once the research in concluded. It is essential for a champion to be brought into the benchmarking process before it starts. Also the champion should be kept up to date on the progress of the research, so, when the result are concluded, he or she will be forewarned and ready to take action. Equally important is checking in—frequently—on the champion's continuing enthusiasm for the project or cause at hand. A champion who is not fully committed to the enterprise may feel "used" for his or her personality or influence among peers. Once duped in some way, a champion can quickly turn that personality and influence into a company's nightmare instead of dream solution.

• *Support from above*: A benchmarking analysis either must be sponsored at the outset by top management in the company or business, or must win top level endorsement once it is conducted. Otherwise, it has relatively little chance of being successfully implemented. Specific ways a top company leader can show his or her support is by frequent public statements (in speeches, newsletters, emails or texts to the workforce, and top agenda items at meetings) as well as open-door discussion opportunities with employees on the issue at hand.

• *Involvement of the right individuals*: It is generally bad practice to conduct a benchmarking analysis of a function without having a variety of individuals from that function -- both those with political power and those with the technical and competitive knowledge -- involved in the process from the start. An outsider may be the catalyst and may conduct a lot of the analysis, but unless he or she has "buy-in" from the key functional managers, those managers are likely to pick apart the analysis at the end rather than support it. Any benchmarking analysis is going to have lots of data which will be questioned by people in the function under study. However, the key is to give them an opportunity to question that data as the process goes along. That way, when the effort is complete, they can focus on the implications of the analysis, rather than question the data.

Step 7: Implement Programs, Monitor Progress and Recalibrate Over Time

To gain the greatest value from your benchmarking efforts, it is crucial to update and monitor the results of the analysis over time. Has your company met the targets that you set for it? Why or why not?

One Japanese competitor has carried this to the extreme. The company has a manufacturing plant which produces over 500 different parts. At one end of the manufacturing plant is a huge bulletin board with a graph for each part indicating targeted cost reductions for each month over a three-year period, as well as actual cost performance. Underneath each of those charts is the name and picture of the individual in the plant who has been assigned responsibility for making sure that that particular part's cost does come down. This system has proven to be a great motivator to ensure that the results of the company's benchmarking effort are in fact carried out. This approach may be too extreme for many American companies, but it illustrates the accountability and follow-through that is characteristic of all good benchmarking processes.

"Sensing systems" are a good way to monitor progress. Top and mid-level managers can be tasked to check in on a regular basis with rank-and-file workers to gain a sense of the workforce on particular issues, including their misgivings and questions. The important aspect of this process is that *something happens* once a worker has voiced a question. The worst blow to any monitoring system is the metaphorical suggestion box that overflows with suggestions but is never emptied and read by upper management.

Successful benchmarking analyses are often "recalibrated" approximately a year later. At that point, any of a number of things may have changed:

• Industry dynamics may have changed in such a way that key success factors have been altered. The performance variables you considered most crucial a year ago therefore may need to be amended.

• New competitors may have entered or may be looming as latent competitors. These competitors need to be added to the analysis. Similarly, you may want to drop some of the other competitors from a year ago, particularly if you found there was little to learn from them by benchmarking their operations. Bear in mind that a latent competitor may be just one lobbyist's winning presentation to a legislator to become an active competitor. Examples are Ford's ceaseless battle to import many of its European brands into the U.S. as high-efficiency/low cost automobiles. More than one tourist to Europe has rented one of these Ford models and asked, "Why aren't these sold in the U.S. (or other country)?" A second example is Japan's on-going effort to protect certain food-products from outside competition. These include rice, certain forms of beef, and half-a-dozen other commodities. All it would take is a new administration in Washington and a tough new deal with Japan to make latent competition into active competition in this case.

• Competitors may have progressed more than you thought they would, so that their costs or other aspects of their performance are better (or worse) than you had projected. You need to update your own targets accordingly. Labor costs are particularly tricky to ascertain in this regard. In Hong Kong, labor costs were historically low for production workers, although not as low as mainland China, India or other parts of Southeast Asia. It comes as a surprise to many visitors, therefore, that IKEA (the furniture giant) does so well in Hong Kong. One expects to turn over any IKEA product and find "Made in China" on the back—but not so. These are Swedish goods, shipped all the way from Sweden to be sold in Hong Kong at a profit. The answer to this financial mystery lies in robotics. Although Swedish workers are well-paid, they are few in number in terms of their per capita productivity. These are the sorts of special factors that must be taken into account when evaluating labor expenses of competitors.

- You also need to measure your own progress relative to your objectives. Have you accomplished in the last year what you said you would, and if not, how should the analysis be amended?

- If your own progress has not been up to standard, you need to identify the cause of the shortfall: were the strategies and actions you recommended the wrong ones, or was the basic strategy correct but there were problems with the execution?

As you conduct benchmarking analyses on an ongoing basis, there is one common pitfall that must be avoided. Companies often forget that while they are improving their operations, competitors are improving as well. An actual but disguised example is shown below, with the year span maintained for accurate context of the period in question.

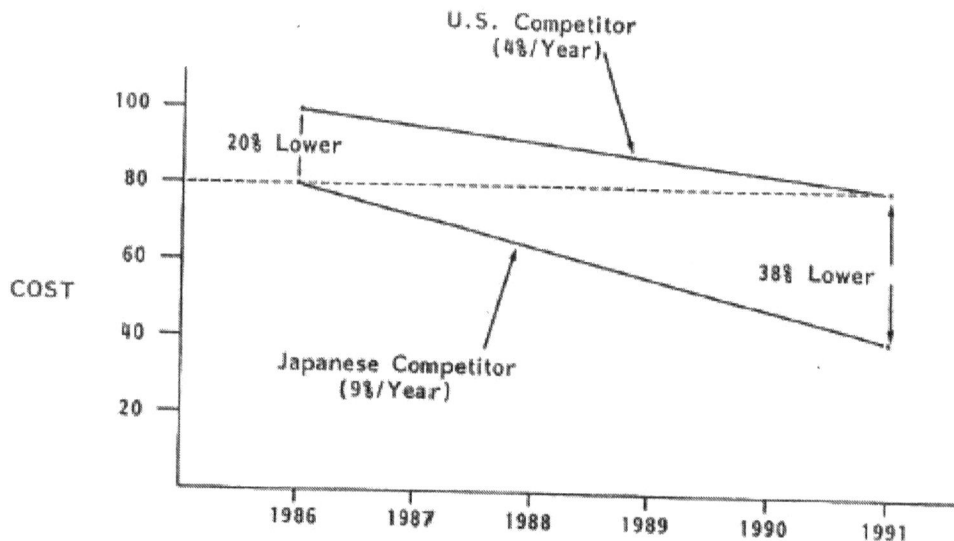

82

Improving Yet Falling Behind

In this example, a U.S. company conducted a benchmarking analysis which identified that its overseas competitor was 20% lower in costs. As the chart shows, the Japanese competitor has a relative cost of "80" while the U.S. competitor had costs of "100." To remedy the situation, the U.S. competitor said it would "aggressively" lower its costs by a little more than 4% per year, so that by 1991 it would be as low cost as the Japanese competitor. What the U.S. competitor omitted from its analysis was consideration of whether the Japanese competitor would be lowering its cost over the same period.

In fact, outside analysis revealed that the Japanese competitor was targeting *9%* cost reduction per year over the same time period, and it had put in place several programs which indicated that this was not an unrealistic objective. If the Japanese competitor succeeded in this cost reduction, by 1991 the Japanese competitor would be 38% lower cost than the U.S. competitor, and the U.S. competitor would be relatively worse off, not better off, than in 1986!

This type of mistake may seem obvious, but it is often made. Companies are so intent on focusing on their own progress that they forget that competitors are moving targets.

Summary

These seven steps apply to almost any benchmarking analysis. However, benchmarking analyses vary widely based on the company, the industry, and the specifics of the situation. The best benchmarking efforts will flexibly weigh the various criteria and rules described above and tailor the analysis to the particular problem being addressed.

Part II:

Strategic

Benchmarking

Chapter 4

Strategic Benchmarking Analysis

As the name suggests, strategic benchmarking identifies significant improvements that can be made to your strategy based on comparisons to best-in-class companies. Those improvements in turn are likely to translate into enhanced financial performance and market position.

The Role of Strategic Benchmarking

Strategic benchmarking is the easier type of benchmarking analysis in terms of the time or resources required. Whereas operational benchmarking can involve very detailed data gathering, strategic benchmarking involves broad but not necessarily exhaustive research and analysis. In strategic benchmarking, the real premium is on understanding the strategy framework discussed in Chapter Two and on a creative and insightful evaluation of the data.

Measuring the value of strategic benchmarking can be a challenge, as unlike operational benchmarking there are generally no obvious metrics. One solution is to 1) talk to senior leaders before the start of the strategic benchmarking program to gather their views on the future of the area to be benchmarked, 2) do the same after the program and 3) compare the two. In some cases, the value may be obvious and quantitative, such as changes in sales growth or company stock price, in others the value may be more subjective and only qualitative. Whichever the result, it is always good to go through the exercise of recording the before and after situations, and building up a record that can be referred to and analyzed at any time in the future.

Despite the fact that strategic benchmarking does not require a large amount of effort, the results can be quite profound and valuable. A number of companies have made major successful changes in their strategy based on relatively straightforward strategic benchmarking efforts, while others have made major mistakes because they have not conducted strategic benchmarking.

Strategic benchmarking is not for everybody. The companies which are likely to benefit the most are those which:

- Have not already conducted high quality competitive and strategic analysis; or

- Find themselves in growing or rapidly changing industries.

Conversely, the following companies may find strategic benchmarking not worth the effort:

- Those which *have* already conducted high quality competitive and strategic analysis;

- Companies in old, slow-moving industries where the competition and the key success factors are already well known and disruptive technologies may have little short term impact like the nuclear power industry, the commercial deep-sea ship building industry, or simply the local dry cleaning market.

A concise but insightful strategic benchmarking effort can be a good first step for a company embarking on a benchmarking program. It should not be skipped over as the exponential increase in computing power is allowing disruptive technologies (3D printing, Artificial Intelligence, robotics, and so forth) to attack any industry.

The Structure of Strategic Benchmarking Analysis

The structure of strategic benchmarking analysis is quite straightforward. Two sets of data are gathered: measurements of the financial and market performance of various competitors in your industry, and description and evaluation of the strategies of those competitors. These sets of data are then correlated to determine the strategies that are producing the best results.

Financial and Market Comparisons

For strategic benchmarking purposes, it is often useful to have a fairly long list of companies in your industry against which to benchmark. The list might include eight to ten competitors as well as your own company. For strategic benchmarking, "best-in-class" companies from outside your industry are not useful as a general rule.

The financial and market data to be gathered may include any or all of the following:

- *Market share data*: What is the market share of each of the competitors in the business? Who has the most share, and who has less? Market share may be measured in either units or dollars, but in general dollars is a much more relevant measure; you can pay the shareholders in dollars but not in units. In general, market share data rounded to the nearest percent, or even the nearest two or three percent, is accurate enough for these purposes.

- *Competitor growth rates*: How have market shares been changing over time? Which competitors have been growing at the fastest rates? Both the market share and the growth data may be gathered for the market as a whole or for various segments, depending upon the scope and purpose of your analysis. Often, share data gathered around three to six segments is detailed enough to generate some interesting insights, but not so detailed as to make the process too cumbersome.

•   *Profitability*: Profit can be measured in a number of ways. The crudest measure of profitability is return on sales, or margin. However, this measure often can yield misleading results about the true profitability of different competitors, as some competitors may be generating a much higher asset turnover than others. Since it is return on investment in assets or equity that the shareholders really want, return on sales by itself is usually too crude a measure of relative profitability. It should be used only when no other data can be gathered or estimated.

Return on assets is a much better measure. Return on assets reflects both the margin, and return on sales of the business, as well as the utilization of assets, or asset turnover. Return on assets data may be gathered on either a pre-tax or post-tax basis. Whereas post-tax data is ultimately more relevant to the shareholder of an individual company, pre-tax data may be at least as useful or even more useful for comparison purposes, since differences in corporate tax rates may cloud the more interesting differences in actual operating profitability.

Return on equity is in theory the best measure of all, since it is the ultimate level of profitability most important to shareholders. However, return on equity is affected significantly by different corporate levels of debt, and this too can often hide actual differences in operating profitability. If return on equity data is used, it is important to check for different levels of debt/equity or debt-to-total-capitalization to make sure that a distortion is not being introduced into the data.

PROFITABILITY MEASURES

MEASURE	DEFINITION
RETURN ON SALES	NET INCOME ÷ SALES
RETURN ON ASSETS	NET INCOME ÷ ASSETS
RETURN ON EQUITY	NET INCOME ÷ EQUITY
OPERATING RETURN ON SALES	OPERATING (Pre-Tax) INCOME ÷ SALES
OPERATING RETURN ON ASSETS	OPERATING INCOME ÷ ASSETS

• *Other measures*: Market share, growth, and profitability measures are often sufficient in capturing the relative success or failure of different competitors in the marketplace. However, you may want to include additional measures: customer satisfaction levels as measured in any available industry surveys or market research; valuation in the stock market, if the competitors you are studying are one-business companies (if the business you are studying is buried deep within the corporation, the corporate stock price may have little relation to the performance of the business in question); or various other measures of success,

SUMMARY: MEASURES OF MARKET AND FINANCIAL PERFORMANCE

MEASURE	COMMENTS
MARKET SHARE	· UNITS OR DOLLARS (preferably dollars)
COMPETITOR GROWTH RATES	· OVERALL GROWTH RATE · GROWTH IN THE VARIOUS MARKET SEGMENTS
PROFITABILITY	· RETURN ON SALES · RETURN ON ASSETS · RETURN ON EQUITY
OTHER	· CUSTOMER SATISFACTION · STOCK VALUATION · OTHERS

It is usually advisable to use a variety of different measures of marketplace and financial success. A common mistake is to use only market share and growth data and to overlook profitability data. By doing so, an analyst may mistake some companies which are fairly large in their markets as successful, when in fact those companies may not have been profitable for years. Both market and financial data must be used to assess which companies truly are the "winners" in your industry.

Benchmarking the Competitors' Strategies

The second set of information to be generated in a strategic benchmarking effort consists of the fundamental strategy of the different competitors in the industry. There is no rigid formula for how to characterize competitor strategies, but the most successful efforts include some or all of the elements described below.

First, you should describe the *overall* strategy of each competitor. A characterization of each competitor's overall strategy might include answers to the following questions:

- What segments of the market is the competitor focusing on?

- Is the competitor pursuing a commodity (low-cost) or specialty (value-added) strategy?

- What level of investment is the competitor making in this market? Is the competitor spending large amounts of money on plants, sales and marketing, R&D, etc., or is the competitor reluctant to allocate its discretionary strategic resources to this business?

- In which functional areas is the competitor deriving its true strength and competitive advantage in the marketplace? Is the competitor differentiating through R&D and technical product superiority? Through manufacturing and low cost production or operations? Through sales, marketing, or customer service, and resultant high customer satisfaction levels? Through strong or proprietary distribution channels? Through superior management or administration?

- What is the competitor's overall strength or weakness in each of the functional areas? Pay particular attention to "under-the-radar" changes and improvements made by your competitors. The classic example of such subtle but effective changes is the dry cleaning chain which quietly expanded their hours, shortened their time to clean garments, and began giving percent discounts for volume amounts of clothes. Within six months, they had increased their net profit by more than 30 percent, with news of the changes coming largely by word of mouth among customers and friendly chat with the affable staff at the various locations. This is the kind of information that is hard to pick up from traditional benchmarking means, but can be crucial in your ultimate analysis of a competitor's strengths and weaknesses, as seen in the following chart.

ELEMENTS OF COMPETITIVE STRATEGY BENCHMARKING

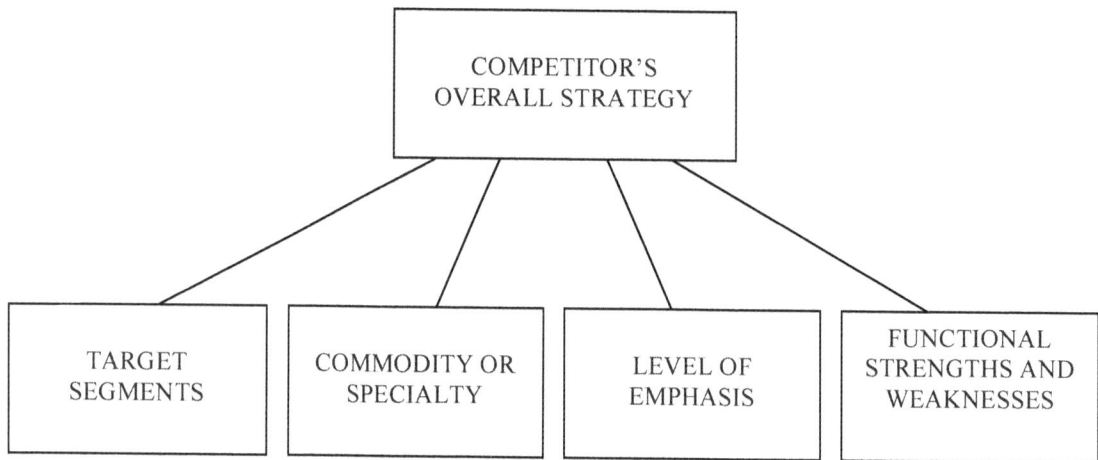

```
                    ┌─────────────────┐
                    │  COMPETITOR'S   │
                    │ OVERALL STRATEGY│
                    └─────────────────┘
```

TARGET SEGMENTS	COMMODITY OR SPECIALTY	LEVEL OF EMPHASIS	FUNCTIONAL STRENGTHS AND WEAKNESSES

At the next level of depth, the characterization of each competitor's strategy should include what the competitor is actually doing in <u>each</u> *functional area*. Examples of questions which might be addressed for each of the functional areas include:

• *Research and development/engineering*: What is the competitor's relative focus on product R&D versus process (or manufacturing / operations) R&D? Product R&D will translate into improved product in the marketplace, while process R&D may result in lower cost. Is the R&D effort focused on a couple of key areas, or spread over a wide range of areas? Which areas? What is the overall level of spending on R&D, relative to sales or revenue?

- *Manufacturing*: What is the competitor's level of vertical integration? Does the competitor make or buy various key components, subassemblies, and assemblies? Where does the competitor manufacture and what is the labor cost in the different areas? Does the competitor utilize large plants with broad product lines or "focused factories"? How automated is the competitor's manufacturing process?

- *Operations*: Operations is the function analogous to manufacturing for service companies. Questions might include: How automated is the competitor's service function? What level, skill, and experience-base of personnel is manning the firm's operations? Are operations centralized or decentralized? The answers to some of these key questions may be obscured by outside factors. For example, farm subsidies in the U.S. pay farmers for not growing crops under some circumstances. The money farmers receive is sufficient to keep on their regular workforce so that, when planting season returns, they don't have to re-hire. The U.S. Department of Agriculture estimated its 2016 subsidies to farmers at approximately US $7 billion, or about 10 percent of the total aggregate income from all farm products. These government-influenced or government-supported aspects of operations must be included in careful benchmarking.

- *Distribution*: What distribution channels is the competitor using? Does it employ single or multiple channels? Is distribution captive, partially captive, or arms-length? Do distributors have exclusive territories? Do they carry competitors' products?

- *Sales Force*: What is the relative size of the competitor's sales force? What is the relative experience or level of quality of the sales force? Are salesmen providing a consultative function to customers, or merely selling?

- *Marketing*: What is the competitor's relative emphasis on various aspects of the marketing mix? How much advertising is it doing? How much promotion? What are the primary themes of the marketing campaign and of various aspects of the marketing mix? What is the company's pricing strategy?

- *Service*: What level of service does the competitor provide to the customer? Is service provided for free or charged for separately? Are different service levels provided to different customer sets? How much skill do company personnel have in providing service to the customer? What systems are in place to enhance provision of service to the customer?

COMPETITORS' FUNCTIONAL STRATEGIES

FUNCTION	STRATEGIC ISSUES	FUNCTION	STRATEGIC ISSUES
R & D	• Product or process • Broad or focused • Spending relative to sales/revenue	SERVICE	• Level of service • Free or fee-based? • Single or multiple options • Service staff skill levels • Systems
MANUFAC-TURING	• Level of vertical integration • Degree of automation • Labor & materials cost/geographic location of plants • Broad plants or focused factories	INFORMATION TECHNOLOGY (IT)	• Investment level • Types of systems • Strategic value of systems
OPERA-TIONS	• Personnel experience/skill levels • Degree of centralization • Degree of automation	HUMAN RESOURCES	• Company culture • Human Resources policies • Recruitment • Training • Motivation systems
DISTRI-BUTION	• Single vs. multiple channels • Captive vs. arm's length • Exclusive territories	ADMINI-STRATION	• Overall management style • Degree of centralization • Tightness of controls
SALES FORCE	• Size • Experience level • Type of selling	FINANCE	• Working capital management • Physical plant • Tax minimization • Debt levels • Dividend policies
MARKETING	• Marketing mix • Advertising level • Promotion level • Primary themes • Pricing strategy		

• *Information Technology, or IT*: How much investment has the competitor made in IT systems? Where is that investment being applied? What strategic advantages are derived from the IT systems?

- *Human Resources*: What is the company culture? What are the basic human resources policies? 'How are people recruited, trained, motivated, and compensated?

- *Administration*: What style of administration does the company practice? Are decisions made centrally or on a de-centralized basis? How tight are controls?

- *Finance:* How aggressive are the company's financial policies? How much profit is the company squeezing out of streamlined inventories or receivables, streamlined physical plant, or aggressive tax minimization? What are the company's debt and dividend policies?

Correlating the Data

You are now ready for the final step. The market and financial performance data enable you to identify the true winners and losers in the marketplace. You then look for those aspects of the competitors' strategies that correlate most closely with successful performance. Often, you will find that aspects of strategy that were thought to be important are just not present in the competitors that are most successful. At the same time, the correlation is likely to identify key elements of strategy that are crucial for success. A well thought out analysis is likely to yield significant recommendations for how your own strategy should be altered to maximize your chances of future success.

Chapter 5

Examples of Strategic Benchmarking

The examples below include only highlights and summary results; the underlying analyses have been drastically simplified. Nonetheless, these examples illustrate the basic nature of strategic benchmarking.

An Example by Default: The Information Industry

As indicated in the RIM example in Chapter 1, the mobile market provides an excellent example of the dangers of failing to undertake strategic benchmarking. As discussed above, RIM continued to play in this market without a good fundamental understanding of what it took to win in the business. However, a basic strategic benchmarking analysis could have helped the company avoid its disastrous collapse in market share that followed it switching its strategic corporate focus away from cellphone market to attack the tablet market in 2011.

The first interesting piece of data would have surfaced from a financial analysis. The numbers for 2010 shown below indicate the dominance of Apple, key Asia companies and RIM in managing profitable businesses. In 2010, just before RIM made its fateful move into the tablet market, it was the most profitable of all players. However other players were hurting with both LG and Motorola have low single digit pre-tax profit levels. For Motorola, this resulted in them splitting the company and selling the cell phone operations off to Google in 2011 under the name of Motorola Mobility, with the result that Motorola transferred itself from a loss making competitor to one making nearly a 30% ROE as part of Google, and surpassing even Apple.

A detailed financial benchmarking would have allowed RIM to drill down and see where the high profits of Apple, HTC and Samsung resided in their product mix, as all had multiple product lines. When we add in the same financial for 2012, we see a very different picture, with Apple increasing its profitability, Motorola's loss being replaced by Google's massive profitability, RIM and HTC loosing profitability and Nokia going into the red. These financials clearly point to who have been the winners and losers in these short two years, plus the volatility and, hence, sensitivity of this market to competitive forces.

PROFITABILITY OF SELECTED DATA IT COMPANIES

COMPANY	2010 ROE	2012 ROE
RIM (U.S.)	22%	8%
APPLE (U.S.)	21%	27%
HTC (Taiwan)	16%	6%
SAMSUNG (S Korea)	12%	12%
LG (S Korea)	1%	1%
MOTOROLA (U.S.)	3%	
GOOGLE (new owner of MOTOROLA MOBILITY)		29%
NOKIA (Sweden)	4%	-9%
INDUSTRY AVERAGE	11%	11%
U.S. INDUSTRIAL AVERAGE	16%	21%

Note: the ROE data above for 2010 vs. 2012 is intended to correlate with the explanations that follow in this chapter. The data is intended as a mini-case study, not as a current statement of profitability. An analysis of the relative strengths of each competitor would illustrate the reasons for these differences. The chart below summarizes the strengths and weaknesses of each competitor in each of several key functional areas. Although not illustrated here, the functional area of Governmental and Regulatory Factors must be continuously monitored as a key aspect influencing functional areas, especially when making cross-country comparisons.

FUNCTIONAL STRENGTHS & WEAKNESSES
OF SMART PHONE COMPETITORS

COMPANY	R & D	MANUFACTURING	SALES	SERVICE
APPLE smartphone	HIGH	MEDIUM	HIGH	HIGH
APPLE tablet	HIGH	MEDIUM	HIGH	HIGH
RIM smartphone	HIGH	MEDIUM	HIGH	HIGH
RIM – tablet	LOW	MEDIUM	LOW	LOW
MOTOROLA	MEDIUM	MEDIUM	LOW	LOW
NOKIA	HIGH	MEDIUM	LOW	LOW
SAMSUNG – smart phone	HIGH	HIGH	HIGH	MEDIUM
SAMSUNG – tablet	HIGH	HIGH	HIGH	MEDIUM
LG	HIGH	HIGH	MEDIUM	MEDIUM
HTC	MEDIUM	HIGH	MEDIUM	MEDIUM

The correlation between the successful table competitors – Apple and Samsung–and strength in sales and service is very strong. On the other hand, manufacturing cost and R&D were not important determinants of success; and companies that were strong in those areas were not guaranteed good levels of marketplace and strong financial profitability. As described in the opening chapter, RIM expanded into the tablet market and based its strategy on its manufacturing and R&D, while ignoring its weak tablet product functionality, which directly impacted sales and service. At the same time, it turned its back on its prime product, the smart phone, just when competitors were aggressively investing in new designs and increasing their profitability. A very basic strategic benchmarking analysis would have raised serious doubts about RIMs strategy, and could have prevented the billions of dollars of losses that followed.

Example: Heavy Duty Truck Components

An example of a company that identified a range of different strategy options based on its benchmarking effort is provided by a company that makes heavy duty truck components for truck manufacturers. In this case there are nine competitors, with market and financial strengths as summarized in the chart below.

HEAVY-DUTY TRUCK COMPONENT COMPETITORS

COMPETITOR	MARKET SHARE	GROWTH RATE	PRE-TAX RETURN ON ASSETS
A	6%	0%	6%
B	7%	11%	13%
C	4%	4%	10%
D	3%	9%	8%
E	11%	8%	14%
F	2%	5%	12%
G	15%	12%	15%
H	10%	(2%)	5%
I	1%	4%	8%

Three of the companies -- B, E, and G -- are clearly the winning competitors, in terms of market and financial measures.

The next chart ranks the relative strength of the competitors in three key functional areas.

RANKING OF COMPETITORS IN TERMS OF FUNCTIONAL STRENGTHS

(1 = Weakest, 10=Strongest)

COMPETITOR	PRODUCT DEVELOPMENT	LOW-COST MANUFACTURING (10 = lowest cost)	CUSTOMER SERVICE
A	1	4	1
B	10	6	7
C	8	6	6
D	4	8	5
E	5	8	10
F	2	8	6
G	3	10	4
H	7	3	5
1	3	3	6

As noted in the chart, there is more than one winning strategy in this industry. Competitor G succeeds through being the low-cost manufacturer. Competitor B succeeds by being the leader in product innovation. Finally, Competitor E succeeds by having the best customer service. The other six competitors are not distinctive in any area. Competitor D, which is the company that conducted this analysis, concluded that it must develop superior strength in one of those three areas in order to significantly improve its financial and market performance. After careful consideration, Competitor D decided that achieving a low cost position was its best bet, and focused its strategic resources on achieving that objective

Example: Yahoo and Google in Search

In the global search market, Google had a 67% market share in mid-2013, compared to Yahoo with 18%, Microsoft with 11%, leaving 4% for all the others. As can been see from the table below, both Google and Yahoo are highly profitable, but their strategies differ significantly. Yahoo does not have its own search technology but uses Microsoft Bing, unlike Google which has been the leader in home-developed search ever since it launched.

Unlike Google, Yahoo has set itself up as web portal. In addition, it has made some strategic investments, like investing in the Chinese online retailer, Alibaba, which netted in $4.6 billion in profits in 2012 when it sold some of its holding and, in 2014, it acquired the popular photo sharing website, Tumbler.

COMPARATIVE PROFITABILITY OF SEARCH

	2010-2012 AVERAGE	
	OPERATING MARGIN	ROE
YAHOO (excluding share trading in Alibaba)	33%	17%
GOOGLE	34%	25%

A strategic benchmarking analysis indicated that the two companies had different strategies and yet comparably strong results.

SUMMARY OF FUNCTIONAL STRATEGY BENCHMARKS

	YAHOO	GOOGLE
SEARCH TECHNOLOGY	OUT-SOURCED	IN-HOUSE
CONTENT	INFORMATION PORTAL	SEARCH PORTAL
KEY CONTENT	FINANCIAL	MAPS
E-MAIL	IN-HOUSE & IM	IN-HOUSE
ADVERTISING	SIGNIFICANT	SIGNIFICANT

The two companies had designed and implemented strong, internally consistent strategies at opposite ends of the spectrum. The other major player in the search market, Microsoft does not break out its financials for search, but it is recognized that it has spent a considerable amount of R&D developing its own search engine without it being profitable. At the end of 2013, Microsoft's CFO stated that profitability was just round the corner. Compared to the other two giants in the market, Microsoft is a very poor third as a simple benchmarking shows. An important Yahoo footnote for 2016 involves a massive data breach for 500 million user accounts that occurred in 2014 but was not confirmed by the company until September, 2016. Another hack attack, this time involving at least 1 billion user accounts, took place in December, 2016. Earlier in that same year, Yahoo Games—once the go-to hub for online card- and board-games—shut down operations. All this technological, operational, and financial turmoil was occurring at a time when Yahoo was publicly advertising itself for sale, a purchase made in late July, 2016, by Verizon for a lackluster US $5 billion, far from the valuation of the internet company in previous years.

Part III:

Operational Benchmarking

Chapter 6

The Types of Operational Benchmarking

Operational benchmarking focuses on a specific aspect of a company's functional, operations, and identifies ways to achieve "best-in-class" status in those operational areas. It is the more demanding form of benchmarking to perform, both in terms of the detail of data to be gathered and the rigor of analysis. It is also more commonly conducted than strategic benchmarking.

Operational benchmarking analyses take a wide variety of forms. In general, the different types of operational studies can be segmented along two dimensions.

First, an operational benchmarking effort can focus on either <u>cost</u> or "*differentiation*" or both. The reason for this is very basic. The fundamental goal of any business is to make a superior profit. The simplest formula for profitability is: Profit = Price - Cost. In order to contribute to superior profitability, a benchmarking effort must identify ways for you to raise price by differentiating your offering in the marketplace, or it must identify ways for you to reduce your costs.

Although this principle is simple, it is remarkable how often it is ignored in the formulation of business plans and competitive analysis. For example, many business plans begin by describing the overall environment and conclude that the market is increasingly competitive and that things are getting tough. They then describe the strategies of the various competitors, all of whom are going to be aggressive. Third, they go on to describe "our own" strategy, articulating the many tactical steps the business will take over the ensuing year.

Finally, they end with "pro-forma" financial projections, showing that profits will be much better in the future than they have been in the past.

In reviewing the accuracy and usefulness of such a plan, it is helpful to ask a couple of questions. First, based on the various actions you are planning to take, are you now going to be lower cost than the competition? Often, the answer is that no, competitors are also striving to reduce their costs, and while we have to do these things to stay in the ballpark, we cannot expect to be lower cost than the competition. Second, based on the various tactical actions you plan to take, will you be able to differentiate yourselves in the marketplace so that you can sell your product at a price premium? In many markets, the answer is again no, because it is a competitive market, and you have to sell at the same price as everyone else.

If you put these various facts together, they are not internally consistent. The overall industry profitability is going to be under pressure, we are going to sell at the same price as everyone else and produce at the same cost as everyone else, but somehow we are going to have superior profitability. This violates the very simple equation stated above.

One of the major differences between good planning efforts and less valuable ones is the degree of rigor with which the equation described above is applied. Until you have formulated a strategy that enables you to produce at a lower cost or differentiate your offering in order to sell at a superior price, you are doomed to the industry average profitability. And the simple fact of the matter is that for most industries today the average profitability is not satisfactory. Good planning efforts are not finished until a strategy for superior price or lower cost has been developed.

For this reason, operational benchmarking efforts typically focus on either or both of the two variables:

- Competitive cost;

- Competitive differentiation (and price).

Operational benchmarking identifies ways to achieve superiority in at least one of those two areas in order to attain superior profitability.

A second dimension distinguishing the various types of operational benchmarking efforts consists of the function or functions to be benchmarked. Operational benchmarking efforts focus on engineering, manufacturing, sales, or some other function or combination of functions. In any of these functions, you can seek ways to reduce cost or to contribute to the differentiation of your company's offering in the marketplace.

The first step in your operational benchmarking effort is to decide which of these various types of operational benchmarking will be most valuable for your operation. Although benchmarking of any function can be valuable, the key is to pick the analysis which offers the biggest "bang for the buck". The criteria for selecting the type of benchmarking are described in Chapter 3.

The remainder of Part IV focuses first on cost benchmarking, and then on benchmarking of differentiation. Both of these approaches can be applied to any function in the value-added chain.

The Value Chain

The concept of a value chain was given succinct description and visualization by Michael Porter in his 1985 book, *Competitive Advantage: Creating and Sustaining Superior Performance*. In essence, a value chain is an organized, orderly set of activities performed by a company with the goal of producing and delivering to the customer a product or service that has value for that marketplace. Some of these activities are viewed as "primary," in the sense that they make up the core processes of developing and delivering the product or service. Primary activities of a company include Inbound Logistics, Operations, Outbound Logistics, Marketing and Sales, and Service. Lacking any one of these, the Value Chain is broken and the prospect of producing and selling the end product or service is destroyed. Other company activities, including Organization, Human Resource Management, Technological Development and Purchasing, are variously termed "support" or "secondary" in nature. As shown I the following chart, these support functions align with each of the primary activities of the company throughout the value chain process. A primary activity such as Marketing and Sales can be devastated by the absence or poor performance of a necessary support activity such as appropriate Technology or Human Resource Management.

PORTER'S VALUE CHAIN

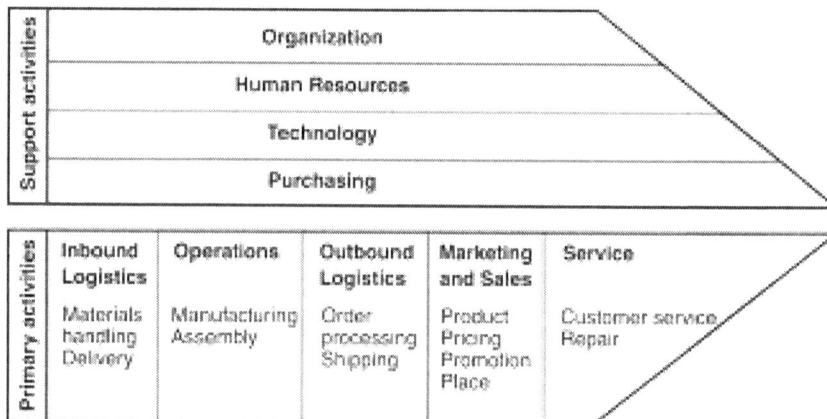

	Inbound Logistics	Operations	Outbound Logistics	Marketing and Sales	Service
	Materials handling Delivery	Manufacturing Assembly	Order processing Shipping	Product Pricing Promotion Place	Customer service Repair

Support activities: Organization, Human Resources, Technology, Purchasing

An Example of a Value Chain: Starbucks

Beginning with just one store in Seattle in 1971, Starbucks has grown to one of the most familiar brands on earth. With more than 22,000 retail operations in 70 countries, the company relies upon a strict and consistent value chain to achieve its mission "to inspire and nurture the human spirit—one person, one cup and one neighborhood at a time."

Consider the primary activities that lie behind and make possible the same reliable products and service across Starbucks vast marketplace.

Primary Activities

Inbound Logistics

Unlike many of its competitors, Starbucks does not subcontract the procurement of coffee beans, the heart of its eventual product. Green, unroasted coffee beans are purchased by Starbucks coffee buyers from well-managed, quality farms in Africa, Asia, and Latin America. Starbucks oversees the roasting of these beans and their eventual packaging and transport to distribution centers for shipping to regional and eventually local coffee outlets.

Operations

With operations in 70 countries and more than 22,000 retail outlets, Starbucks does business under the trademark banners of Starbucks Coffee, Teavana, Seattle's Best Coffee and Evolution Fresh. Approximately 80 percent of retail stores are owned outright by Starbucks, with the remainder operated under licensing agreements.

Outbound Logistics

Starbucks does not use "middle-men" in selling its products. The efficiency of its value chain ensures that the right types and amounts of coffee and other products are delivered directly to the retail outlets for point-of-sale "final processing" by well-trained company barristas. Knowledgeable staff, from the cashiers to the store manager, are prepared by the company to sell specialty and bulk coffee items, including exotic coffee beans from Rwanda, Timor, and remote regions of Guatemala. Coffee-brewing equipment, since 2016, has been a best-seller for Starbucks, even though it equips a customer with the ability to brew his or her own "Starbucks coffee" at home rather than visiting a local Starbucks store.

Marketing and Sales

Unlike some of its competitors, Starbucks invests relatively little in media advertising other than its omnipresent retail signs. Instead, the company focuses on delivering prompt, friendly service and top-quality products in environments conducive to computer work, reading, or simply chatting with friends and new acquaintances. This "coffee house" culture goes far in stimulating word-of-mouth recommendations to others from satisfied customers who feel they have been "served, not sold."

Service

Starbucks repeats in each of its annual reports its aim "to be the leading retailer and brand of coffee in each of our target markets by selling the finest quality coffee and related products, and by providing each customer a unique *Starbucks Experience*." To achieve this goal, store managers are tasked with the responsibility of monitoring interaction between store employees and customers—and to act quickly in the event that an employee is not living up to the Starbucks culture and code.

Support Activities

Infrastructure

While not all Starbucks stores have identical layouts, the similar "look" of a store's serving line and coffee pick-up location is apparent, as are the green-aproned employees. Other "backroom" functions involving finance, record-keeping, employee training, and so forth are largely hidden from the customer's view. All aspects of each store, from comfortable furniture to clean restrooms, are calculated to support "the Starbucks Experience."

Human Resource Management

Starbucks leads its industry in employee pay, incentives, and benefits. As a consequence, it has one of the lowest turnover rates in the coffee-house sector, resulting in well-trained, experienced employees who know how to handle virtually any issue or problem in the store. The company invests substantially in on-going training programs for all employees, further increasing their loyalty and motivation.

Technology Development

Starbucks has become legendary as a place to do personal or group business due to its free and fast wifi availability, choices of table and chairs or over-stuffed, "living-room" seating, and a constant emphasis on store cleanliness. **Starbucks has led the way in its industry with regard to convenient customer "apps," including smart phone downloads for ordering coffee before getting to the store and paying for it electronically.**

Procurement

Starbucks employs expert coffee agents to seek out the highest grade coffee throughout the world. Relationships are built up for the long term by the company with reliable suppliers who meet the company's high standards for treatment of employees. Starbucks is constantly in the business of quality control, making sure that the coffee beans they buy translate successfully into a product worth $3.50 to $6 to customers. In procuring the best coffee beans available, Starbucks makes use of its own buying channels in preference to purchasing beans on the open market.

The Value of the Value Chain

As a pattern for organized business activity, the value chain for Starbucks (and other companies who employ this approach) provides not only a template for running the business at a profit but also for trouble-shooting company problems when they emerge. If, for example, customer feedback (through Starbucks on-line site for this purpose) indicates lack of customer satisfaction in some aspect of the Starbucks Experience, managers can look to the Value Chain to determine where the breakdown is occurring and how it can best be repaired. The company can also increase the value of its end product and service by ramping up the goals and efficiency of each aspect of the Value Chain. The following chart provides a handy checklist of various aspects of company processes, including their relative cost and advantages of differentiation. Used with Porter's Value Chain, this kind of analytic instrument can sharpen a company's focus on what matters most to the quality and profitability of the end product or service.

SUMMARY: TYPES OF OPERATIONAL BENCHMARKING

TYPE OF COMPETITIVE ADVANTAGE / FUNCTION (Examples)	COST	DIFFERENTIATION	
R & D/ENGINEERING			
MANUFACTURING/OPERATIONS			
SALES			
MARKETING			
DISTRIBUTION			
INFORMATION TECHNOLOGY			
SERVICE			
ADMINISTRATION			

Chapter 7

Activity Based Costing

Over the last several years, cost benchmarking, now known as Activity Based Costing (ABC), has been by far the most commonly performed type of benchmarking. Given the pressure on many companies to increase profitability, the entry of new, low-cost competition, and the historical tendency of some companies to develop large bureaucracies, many companies are looking for ways to increase their competitiveness via significant reduction in cost.

Activity based costing can be a major catalyst in helping companies reduce costs. When companies consider where they can reduce headcount or other costs, there is usually tremendous resistance from individual functional organizations and managers. There is a feeling that "we are already doing things as efficiently as possible, and there's no way we can be any leaner than we already are."

Through activity based costing, data is gathered on other companies, revealing how some of them are running the same functions as your company with less cost and/or fewer people. This data can open some eyes and challenge traditional thinking about your own company's efficiency.

There's nothing magical about the way activity based costing is done. There's no secret formula or secret way to get data. There is really only one trick to the process, and that is on setting your sights on the right type of data to perform the comparison between the best-in-class companies and your own organization.

Specifically, the way *not* to approach activity based costing is to try to get your cost accounting statement and your competitor's cost accounting statement and compare the two. First of all, your competitor's cost accounting statement is just not available through any legal or ethical means. Second of all, even if you had it, it would not likely be sufficient because it will be based on a different set of assumptions and methodology than your cost accounting system.

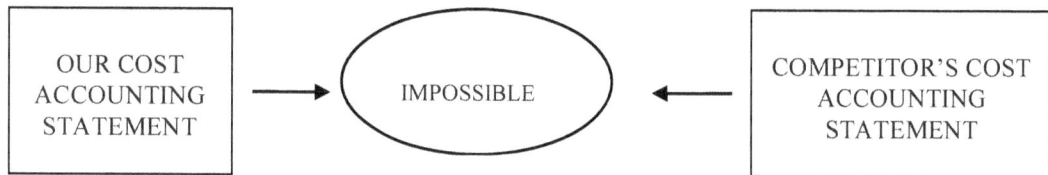

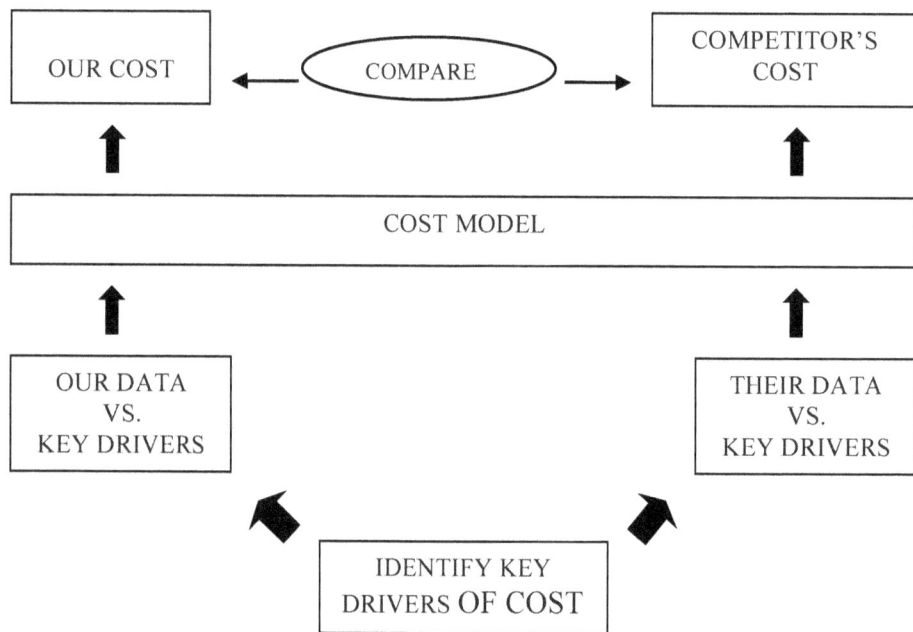

```
┌──────────────┐         ╭─────────────╮         ┌──────────────────┐
│  OUR COST    │  ───▶   │             │   ◀───   │ COMPETITOR'S COST│
│  ACCOUNTING  │         │  IMPOSSIBLE │          │   ACCOUNTING     │
│  STATEMENT   │         │             │          │   STATEMENT      │
└──────────────┘         ╰─────────────╯         └──────────────────┘
```

```
┌──────────┐     ╭──────────╮     ┌──────────────┐
│ OUR COST │ ◀── │ COMPARE  │ ──▶ │ COMPETITOR'S │
│          │     ╰──────────╯     │    COST      │
└──────────┘                      └──────────────┘
      ▲                                  ▲
┌──────────────────────────────────────────────────┐
│                   COST MODEL                      │
└──────────────────────────────────────────────────┘
      ▲                                  ▲
┌──────────────┐                  ┌──────────────┐
│  OUR DATA    │                  │  THEIR DATA  │
│     VS.      │                  │     VS.      │
│ KEY DRIVERS  │                  │ KEY DRIVERS  │
└──────────────┘                  └──────────────┘
         ◤                          ◥
            ┌──────────────────┐
            │ IDENTIFY KEY     │
            │ DRIVERS OF COST  │
            └──────────────────┘
```

The trick is to express your own cost in terms of some fundamental underlying cost "drivers" which are relatively pure in terms of the way in which they are defined. You then go out and get similar data for the cost drivers for the best-in-class firms. Once that data is gathered, you model actual costs based on the cost driver data, and arrive at a comparison between your cost and the competitor's cost.

One of the endemic hidden costs in this sort of analysis can be termed the "King Tut" phenomenon—that is, the temptation to build a temple bearing the company name and, through accounting maneuvers, keep its cost and maintenance from being adequately reflected in an apples-for-apples comparison with competitors. Every major city bears evidence of this tendency on the part of major companies to "go big" in the city skyline and to worry about how the mammoth building will actually be used for business purposes at a later date. The graveyard of companies who have "built before they analyzed" is crowded indeed. Consider the millions of square feet of empty Target stores across the width of Canada as a recent example. The company projected its respectable success in the U.S. market to what it believed to be a similar population in Canada. Obviously, the analysis was flawed, and expensively so. Canadians undisposed to frequenting what they perceived as an American outsider complained of empty shelves in the Target stores during the roll-out period, a paucity of Canadian-made goods, and prices that were no bargain when compared with "their own" box stores such as Canadian Tire. To their credit, Target saw the handwriting on the wall and simply pulled the plug on the whole Canadian venture. Virtually no analysis showed them how they could win against the cultural and existing competitive factors pitted again them.

ACTIVITY BASED COSTING IN COMPETITIVE ENVIRONMENTS

The best cost drivers have the following characteristics:

- They are defined in a straightforward way, so that they are relatively consistent among companies;

- Data for them is available from competitors as well as your own company;

- They capture most of the cost of a given company activity or function. For example, the activity cost for the sales function is usually largely people cost, and therefore various cost drivers that together reflect people cost capture most of the cost of the function. Those drivers may not capture the cost of the telephone bill or the money spent on office supplies, but on the other hand, those latter costs are a relatively small part of total cost and are relatively insignificant

The benefits of using activity cost drivers are two-fold, and both are very powerful:

• It is really the only way the analysis can be done, for the reasons stated above. You often cannot get actual cost data for your competitors.

• Even more important, modeling costs through use of activity cost drivers enables you to arrive at a dual result: not only do you learn how your costs compare to those of your competitors, but you learn why your costs are higher or lower as a function of the various underlying factors or drivers. This makes the information much more useful for developing recommendations on how to reduce your own cost.

Typical Activity Cost Drivers Used

Based on experience with hundreds of activity based costing studies, we have included below numerous examples of cost drivers that companies have found to be useful. However, given the specific nature of your business, there are likely to be others that are important for you as well.

Raw Materials Benchmarks

While it is often difficult to obtain precise raw material costs, enough information can usually be collected to model the significant portions of competitor's raw material cost. For example, if a competitor is purchasing a plastic compound such as polyvinyl chloride (PVC) for thin film packaging, knowing the specific type of PVC purchased, the source (both vendor and plant location), the yearly volume purchased, and the average lot size will enable you to make an excellent estimate of the price paid for the raw material. Much of this data collection and estimation can be done in conjunction with industry suppliers and your own purchasing department.

A key rule of thumb in raw material cost benchmarking is that only major raw material costs should be analyzed. One forest products company analyzed wood costs plus one key chemical that together comprised 95% of total raw material cost. The remaining five percent of cost was assumed to be equal across all competitors.

Sample Raw Materials: Activity Costing Drivers and Benchmarks

- Cost as a percent of sales

- Purchase price/unit

- Yearly purchase volume

- Typical purchase lot size

- Source (domestic vs. foreign, specific location, suppliers)

- Exchange rate trends (if overseas)

- Freight costs

- Duties

- Applicability of "corporate umbrella" purchasing agreements

- Defect rate, other measures of supply quality

- Yield (unit output per unit input)

Direct Labor Benchmarks

Benchmarking direct labor costs is typically relatively straightforward. There are four pieces of data one needs to estimate direct labor costs for a competitor; headcount, wage rates, benefits rates, and volume of production. For example, in benchmarking a competitor's direct labor costs for assembling a bicycle, knowing that each assembler is paid $8.00 per hour, benefits total 22% of base salary, and that a team of two assemblers produces 11 bikes in eight hours, one can calculate a direct labor cost per unit of $14.20. If the bike sells for $100, then we know that direct labor costs are 14.2% of total sales.

2 Assemblers x 8 hours x $8/hour x 1.22 for benefits = $14.20
Labor cost/bike
11 bikes

Practically speaking, direct labor cost benchmarking often takes place at the plant, production line, or department level, rather than at the product level, because product-specific data is often difficult to obtain. For example, a producer of heavy equipment recently gathered headcount data for nine manufacturing departments:

EXAMPLE: ACTIVITY COSTING OF DIRECT LABOR COST

FOUNDRY	MACHINING #1	
· 46	· 251	
· 38	· 220	
· 21%	· 19%	

DIECAST	MACHINING #2	SUB-ASSEMBLY	
· 101	· 411	· 51	ASSEMBLY
· 68	· 337	· 47	· 330
· 49%	· 22%	· 9%	· 329

STAMPINGS	· NO GAP
· 55	
· 33	
· 67%	

SCREW MACHINING
· 40
·37
· 8%

KEY	PAINT & PACK
· Our Headcount/1,000 Units	· 151
· Best-in-Class Headcount/1,000 Units	· 158
· Gap to be Closed, as a Percentage	· NO
	GAP

Based on this information, the company concluded it needed to drastically upgrade its productivity in the diecast and stamping operations, and to achieve some improvement in machining, sub-assembly, and the foundry. It also determined its assembly and paint/pack departments were already as efficient as the best-in-class.

In some cases, headcount data must be "corrected" for differing levels of vertical integration or use of contract or temporary personnel. One service company found that it has 10% more data entry personnel per 1000 transactions than its best-in-class competition. However, further analysis revealed that the competition used more contract labor and, on an apples-to-apples basis, was *not* more productive. Similar corrections must be made to reflect differing levels of vertical integration in manufacturing.

Wage rates can often be obtained directly, from sources such as union contracts or local government surveys. If actual data cannot be obtained, wage rates can be estimated based on factors such as prevailing local wage rates (by county or locality within the U.S.), union vs. non-union status of the workforce, skill levels of the laborers, years of experience on the job, age, and education.

Sample Direct Labor Cost Benchmarks and Drivers

- Cost as a percent of sales

- Headcount

- Hourly wage rates

- Benefits rate

- Exchange rate trends (if overseas)

- Standard weekly hours per worker

- Overtime hours

- Overtime rate

- Unit productivity (units produced per man-hour)

- Revenue productivity (product revenues per man-hour)

- Skilled vs. unskilled labor

- Education levels

- Union vs. non-union labor

- Age and experience l

Indirect Labor Benchmarks

In addition to direct labor, competitors have indirect manufacturing or operations labor, including both supervisory and support personnel. Again, the quantitative data is relatively straightforward: headcount, salaries, benefits rates, and some measure of volume such as units or sales.

In addition to making calculations comparable to those described in the direct manufacturing labor section, it is useful to analyze ratios between indirect and direct labor. Often, two competitors have very different "span of control" ratios, supervisors-to-direct-employees. These differences may reflect different efficiencies, different operating philosophies, or both. One analysis a number of years ago showed that Radio Shack had two fewer layers of regional store management than AT&T's Phone Stores, despite having seven times as many stores. The analysis revealed that AT&T was not getting commensurate benefits from those added layers of management and therefore had a real indirect labor cost problem.

Sample Indirect Labor Benchmarks and Drivers

- Overall cost as percent of sales

- Headcount

- Management-to-direct labor

- Direct-labor-to-support

- Salary levels

- Benefits rates

- Exchange rate trends (if overseas)

- Unit productivity (units produced per man-hour)

- Revenue productivity (product revenues per man-hour)

- Education levels

- Union vs. non-union labor

- Age and experience levels

Sales Cost Benchmarks

In most industries, the majority of sales cost differences can be explained through an analysis of personnel costs; non-personnel costs are often minor.

One critical sales benchmark is dollar volume per salesperson. In many industries, the amount of revenues generated by the average salesman differs significantly across companies. Critical benchmarks affecting salesforce productivity include: years of experience, compensation plan (straight versus variable compensation), quotas, number of accounts handled, average account size, sales calls per day, and time spent on activities other than direct selling.

In addition to benchmarking direct salesforce productivity, it is often useful to analyze the level of sales support companies are offering their sales teams. For example, one can compare levels of investment in telephone-based customer service reps, technical support reps, and clerical staff.

Benchmarking of sales force compensation usually includes a number of factors: salary, commissions or bonuses, the basis for that incentive compensation, and benefits.

Sample Sales Cost Benchmarks and Drivers

- Overall cost as percent of sales

- Overall sales organization headcount

- Revenue productivity (revenues per direct salesperson)

- Types of salespeople (e.g., national accounts, regional, industry specialists)

- Ratio of sales support to direct sales personnel

- Ratio of management to direct sales personnel

- Salary levels

- Compensation/incentive plan

- Benefits rates

- Quotas

- Average number of accounts per salesperson

- Sales calls per day

- Sales calls per account per year

- Turnover rate

- Education levels

- Age and experience levels

- Sales training and recruiting

- Cost of literature and samples

- Travel benefits, including keeping airline "points"

R&D. Marketing, and Administration Cost Benchmarks

Research and development (or engineering), marketing, and administrative functions are driven in large part by labor costs. Benchmarking of headcount, salary, and benefits data therefore captures much of cost. Most benchmarking of these areas focuses not only on the total amount of labor, but also on the division of labor among differing areas of responsibility.

For example, most benchmarking analyses of the R&D or engineering areas typically divide personnel among categories such as:

- Basic R&D

- New product development

- Refinements of existing products

- Cost reduction engineering

- Applications engineering

Similarly, marketing staff is usually separated among a number of categories, including marketing research, product management, advertising, promotion, and other categories.

Administrative personnel are typically divided into a wide range of categories, including areas such as IT (further divided into system analysts, system designers, software developers, maintenance, web and mobile support services, etc.), public and/or government relations, accounting, finance, legal, and so forth.

In some cases, cost benchmarking of these areas also includes significant non-personnel expenditures, such as equipment to assist engineers, M.I.S. hardware, or advertising expenditures; however, it is usually not worthwhile to analyze less important cost items such as office supplies, telephone bills, and so forth.

Some of the most significant benchmarking in the U.S. today is being done in the knowledge worker areas. Many companies have found that, while they've been analyzing their manufacturing processes versus those of the competition for years, their knowledge worker functions are viewed as "overhead" and have received very little scrutiny. Many of the companies that have recently announced major reductions in force of their knowledge worker employees have done so as the result of good benchmarking analyses.

As a case in point, according to Bloomberg.com (Jan. 13, 2016), GE carefully benchmarked the costing implications in its acquisition of Alstom SA, particularly with regard to justifiable layoffs it could make of redundant workers in its European operations. Over the course the ot the next decade, GE expects to see a US $3 billion savings from its reduction of 6,500 Europe workers.

Sample R&D. Marketing, and Administration Cost Benchmarks and Drivers

- Overall cost of each function as percent of sales

- Headcount for each organization

- Headcount breakdown by direct vs. management vs. support

- Headcount break-out by role or specialty of employee

- Percentage of employees tasked with at least one

  innovation goal

- Salary levels

- Bonus plans

- Benefits rates

- Personnel cost to perform a given process

- Systems cost to perform a given process

- Exchange rate trends (if overseas)

- Revenue productivity (revenue per individual in the function)

- Patents per engineer (R&D)

- Drawings per engineer

- Purchase volume per purchasing agent

- Marketing budget as a percentage of revenue

- Sales budget as a percentage of revenue

- Turnover rate

- Education levels

- Age and experience levels

Capital and Fixed Cost Benchmarks

Profitability is driven not only by variable costs but by fixed costs of assets such as plant, equipment and inventories. The more capital intensive the industry, the more critical it is to benchmark fixed costs.

For example, in the airline industry a large portion of cost is the airplane itself, and it is important to benchmark capital invested in airplanes, yearly depreciation or lease costs, and yearly maintenance costs for airplanes. Regardless of volume (e.g., airline passengers), costs remain largely the same and therefore the critical cost driver is some measure of asset utilization (*e.g.,* percentage of seats on the airline filled): the lower the utilization, the higher the fixed cost per unit. Other measures of fixed asset cost include fixed asset turnover and net-fixed-assets-to-gross-fixed-assets (a measure of asset age).

It is frequently important to benchmark the cost of non-fixed assets as well. A traditional measure of inventory cost is simply inventory turnover (defined as yearly cost of goods sold divided by average inventory levels); a company with a high turnover rate is able to maintain low inventories and achieve lower capital costs. Accounts receivable are typically measured by number of days of sales currently uncollected. There are numerous other measures of asset productivity and capital costs unique to specific industries.

Sample Capital Cost Benchmarks and Drivers

- Overall asset turnover (sales/assets)

- Fixed asset turnover

- Fixed asset utilization rates

- Capital expenditures as a percent of net fixed assets (or depreciation)

- Net-fixed-assets-to-gross-fixed assets

- Total cost to manufacture per $1,000 revenue

- Cost of goods sold as a percentage of revenue

- Warranty costs (repair and replacement) as a percentage of sales

- Depreciation rates

- Yearly lease costs

- Maintenance costs

- Inventory turnover

- Days receivable

- Days payable

- Cost of capital

Miscellaneous Cost Benchmarks

Miscellaneous general overhead costs such as rent, executive salaries, or office supplies should be analyzed only if significant. These costs can be estimated by analyzing cost drivers such as square feet of space occupied and cost per square foot (for rent), or total number of top management and general pay scale (for executive salaries). However, one must be sure not to benchmark costs which account for an insignificant level of expenditures. Rather, scarce benchmarking resources are better spent on the major cost elements.

Sample "Miscellaneous" Cost Benchmarks

- Square feet or rent cost as a percent of sales (or per employee)

- Executive compensation as a percent of sales

- Corporate training costs as a percent of sales

- Bad debt expense as percent of sales

- Scrap and rework costs as a percentage of sales

- Warranty expense as percent of sales

Summary: The Steps for Conducting Cost Benchmarking Analyses

To conduct a cost benchmarking analysis, you must:

- Identify your company's cost chain;

- Identify the key drivers for each step of the chain;

- Gather your data for the key drivers;

- Gather the data for the best-in-class for the key drivers;

- Model the cost of the best-in-class;

- Compare to your cost to determine:

    ○ Your relative cost;

    ○ *Where* you are high and low cost;

    ○ *Why* you are high and low cost.

The next two chapters include examples of cost benchmarking analyses. Chapter 8 includes examples of benchmarking of the entire cost chain, while Chapter 9 illustrates cost benchmarking of individual functions.

Chapter 8

Examples of Benchmarking of the Entire Cost Chain

The three examples below illustrate benchmarking of the entire cost chain. These benchmarking efforts are broader than single-function analyses, but do not necessarily require greater effort. Usually, significant insights can be reached without going into any one function in great depth.

Example: Building Materials Cost Benchmarking

In 2015, a mid-size manufacturer of a building material ("Company A") was just completing a major new renovation of an old production facility. As the new facility came on-line, company executives needed to establish concrete goals for minimizing costs in the hotly competitive and price-sensitive market for its product. To meet this objective, the company benchmarked itself against eight of the most profitable competitors in the industry.

Analysis

As the first step, Company A graphically displayed the major components of its own complete cost chain. The chart below portrays those costs. The largest single component of cost was raw material # 1, which accounted for 23.7% of Company A's total cost. The other major costs included raw material #2 (11.8% of total cost), raw material #3 (2.4%), direct labor (5.5%), depreciation (25.2%), other manufacturing costs (20.8%), and sales and administrative costs (10.6%).

For each of these cost elements, a list of cost drivers was identified. For example, there were two cost drivers for raw material #1:

BUILDING MATERIAL COST CHAIN

RAW MATERIAL #3 (2.4)

RAW MATERIAL #1 (23.7% Of Total Cost)	RAW MATERIAL #2 (11.8)	DIRECT LABOR (5.5)	DEPRECIATION (25.2)	OTHER MANUFACTURING COSTS (20.8)	SALES AND ADMINISTRATIVE (10.6)

- The price paid per unit of raw material # 1 purchased. This price was in turn based on the geographic area where the material was purchased, and on lot size;

- The production yield of the raw material, as measured by volume of finished product produced per unit of input of raw material #1.

The chart below shows the final cost calculations for raw material #1. Company B's raw material # 1 cost is 79.3% of Company A's, giving it a bottom line margin advantage of 4.9% of total cost. A quick look at each company indicates that only two companies are higher cost in raw material #1 than Company A (Companies D and F). Each of the other companies has a superior cost position.

Data for the analysis of raw material #1 was gathered from many sources, including published industry price lists and discount schedules (by region), and industry surveys that track production capacity and utilization. A similar methodology was used to compare raw material #2 costs; owing to its small overall impact on cost, the cost of raw material #3 was assumed to be the same for each competitor.

COST OF MATERIAL #1

COMPETITOR	PRICE FACTOR*	YIELD FACTOR*	COST INDEX**	SCALE TO A's 23.7% OF TOTAL COST	DIFFERENCE VS. COMPANY A
A (US)	100.0	100.0	100.0	23.7%	0%
B	83.7	94.7	79.3	18.8	(4.9)
C	102.0	93.4	95.3	22.0	(1.1)
D	111.2	102.8	114.3	27.1	3.4
E	90.8	87.5	79.5	18.8	(4.9)
F	106.1	105.2	111.6	26.4	2.7
G	85.7	102.3	87.7	20.8	(7.6)
H	76.5	88.9	68.0	16.1	(0.6)
I	96.9	30.6	29.7	7.0	(16.7)

* Indexed to A=100

** (Price Factor x Yield Factor* 100)

To estimate competitors' direct labor costs, a different set of cost drivers was used. The four key cost drivers were:

- Number of direct workers in each plant

- Hourly wage rates

- Benefits rates

- Volume of production per hour

From these four pieces of data, comparative direct labor costs were derived by developing a compensation index (first chart below) and a productivity index (second chart below). The results indicate that while Company A has average compensation costs, its productivity compares unfavorably to that of all but one competitor (Company B).

DIRECT LABOR COMPENSATION

COMPETITOR	HOURLY RATE	BENEFITS AS % OF HOURLY RATE	TOTAL COMPENSATION PER HOUR	INDEX
A (US)	$ 7.00	40%	$ 9.80	100.0
B	$ 7.49	39%	$10.41	106.2
C	$ 5.76	39%	$8.00	81.6
D	$ 8.50	39%	$11.81	102.5
E	$ 8.22	32%	$10.85	110.7
F	$ 7.69	35%	$10.38	105.9
G	$ 7.21	34%	$ 9.68	98.3
H	$ 7.20	32%	$ 9.50	96.9
I	$10.00	30%	$13.00	132.6

DIRECT LABOR PRODUCTIVITY

COMPETITOR	NUMBER HOURLY EMPLOYEES	VOLUME OF PRODUCTION PER HOUR	OUTPUT PER HOURLY EMPLOYEE	COST INDEX
A (US)	103	140,000	1,359	100.0
B	175	235,000	1,343	101,2
C	100	147,000	1,470	92.4
D	108	156,000	1,444	94.1
E	205	357,000	1,741	78.1
F	100	147,000	1,470	92.4
G	88	198,000	2,250	60.4
H	155	250,000	1,613	84.2
I	160	320,000	2,000	68.0

The combination of compensation costs and productivity results in an overall direct labor cost disadvantage versus all but two competitors (third chart below). Again, Company A appears to be high cost when compared to the most profitable plants in the industry.

TOTAL DIRECT LABOR COST

COMPETITOR	PRODUCTIVITY INDEX	COMPENSATION INDEX	TOTAL DIRECT LABOR INDEX	INDEX TO A's 5.5 OF TOTAL COST	BOTTOM LINE OVER/(UNDER) COST COMPARISON
A (US)	100.0	100.0	100.0	5.5%	0%
B	101.2	106.2	107.5	5.9	0.4
C	92.4	81.6	75.4	4.1	(1.4)
D	94.1	120.5	113.4	6.2	0.7
E	78.1	110.7	86.5	4.8	(0.7)
F	92.4	105.9	96.3	5.3	(0.2)
G	60.4	98.8	59.7	3.3	(2.2)
H	84.2	96.9	81.6	4.5	(1.0)
I	68.0	132.6	90.2	5.0	(0.5)

Results

The cost benchmarking process was completed for each of the other major cost components, and the results, in index form, are displayed below. Company A found that it was anywhere from 20% to 40% higher cost than the best-in-class companies, in large part due to the high depreciation charges on its new plant. However, even without depreciation (considering only "cash costs"), company A is still a high cost competitor.

TOTAL BUILDING MATERIAL COST COMPENSATION

COMPETITOR	MATERIAL #1	MATERIAL #2	MATERIAL #3	DIRECT LABOR	DEPRECIATION	OTHER MANUFACTURING	S & A	TOTAL
A (US)	23.7%	11.8%	2.4%	5.5	25.2%	20.8%	0.6%	00.0%
B	18. 8	6.6	2.4	5.9	4.8	13.5	.0	1.0
C	22.6	12.1	2.4	4.1	14.2	21.0	.0	4.4
D	27.1	12.8	2.4	6.2	12.3	20.8	.0	9.6
E	18.8	8.9	2.4	4.8	5.7	10.4	.0	7.0
F	26.4	8.4	2.4	5.3	12.6	21.0	.0	4.1
G	20.8	9.3	2.4	3.3	4.8	20.8	0.0	1.4
H	16.1	12.4	2.4	4.5	8.6	13.5	.0	6.5
I	7.0	33.7	2.4	5.0	13.3	10.4	.5	9.3

In addition to the above cost analysis, an analysis of how each competitor achieved lower costs was conducted. This analysis highlighted technological, manufacturing process, and management policy differences between competitors, and it identified high impact actions that Company A could take to reduce its costs.

The above example portrays the type of creative "mechanics" that an analyst must develop to complete an entire cost chain benchmarking analysis. In the next example, we will bypass the mechanics, but show how benchmarking of the entire cost chain provided the roadmap for turning around an unprofitable operation.

Example: Banking Industry Activity Based Costing

Many commercial banks have recently faced increasing profit pressure as the result of deregulation and the "blurring" of competitive boundaries. In particular, small commercial banks have recently had to withstand entry into their local markets by large regional banks and by national, money center banks. One small local bank had been quite profitable for twenty years and had never seriously considered the impact of competition. However, in recent years, three larger institutions had penetrated the market and significantly reduced the profit levels previously enjoyed by the small bank.

To combat the slide in profits, the small regional bank had originally decided that it must expand to new geographic regions and into new product areas. But before these expansion plans were put in place, the company benchmarked its entire cost structure versus those of the three large competitors. The benchmarking effort resulted in a significant change in strategy.

Analysis

The chart below depicts the overall cost structure of the small bank

SMALL BANK'S TOTAL COST CHAIN

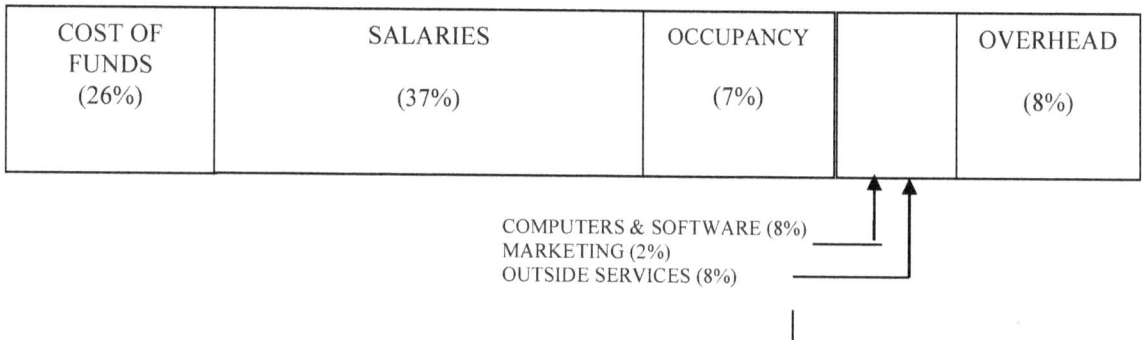

COST OF FUNDS (26%)	SALARIES (37%)	OCCUPANCY (7%)		OVERHEAD (8%)

COMPUTERS & SOFTWARE (8%)
MARKETING (2%)
OUTSIDE SERVICES (8%)

COST DRIVERS: • Mix of fund sources
     -- Non-interest demand deposits
     -- Interest bearing deposits
     -- Short-term borrowings
     -- Long-term borrowings
     • Rates paid for each source of funds

• Number of branches
• Average branch size
• Number of ATM's
• Number of accounts

Clearly, the largest component of cost was the cost of funds. Funds were of essentially four types:

- Demand deposits (non-interest bearing)

- Interest bearing deposits

- Short-term borrowings from other institutions

- Long-term borrowings

Each of the sources of funds carried a different cost. For example, while demand deposits paid no interest, interest bearing deposits cost roughly 8%, short-term borrowings 8.7%, and long-term borrowings over 10%.

A benchmarking of both the mix of funds and the rates paid (chart below) showed that the small regional bank's overall cost of funds was 50 to 100 basis points above that of its regional rivals -- an 8% to 15% cost disadvantage. The analysis showed that the small bank's comparatively low level of demand deposits coupled with high short and long-term borrowing rates were the source of the cost of funds disadvantage. The small bank needed to significantly improve its cost of funds in order to remain cost competitive.

COST OF FUNDS BENCHMARKING

	NON-NTEREST BEARING DEPOSITS	INTEREST BEARING DEPOSITS	SHORT-TERM BORROWED FUNDS	LONG-TERM BORROWED FUNDS	WEIGHTED AVERAGE COST OF FUNDS
SMALL BANK	Rate = 0 % of Funds=15	8.02% 75%	8.68% 9%	10.7% ‹ 1%	6.83%
MID-SIZE REGIONAL BANK	0% 19%	7.90% 64%	9.94% 16%	8.57% 1%	6.39%
LARGE REGIONAL BANK	0% 28%	7.83% 57%	8.02% 14%	10.22% 1%	5.69%
NATIONAL BANK	0% 9%	8.58% 47%	8.71% 28%	11.10% 16%	8.20%

The small bank also benchmarked operating costs not related to the acquisition of funds. The bank found that it compared favorably to one competitor but was higher cost than the other two. Further detailed analysis of operating costs revealed areas in which the small bank could reduce cost through a series of different actions, including the elimination and re-sizing of some of its branches.

Results

The small bank learned from the experience and cost structure of its larger competitors. The small bank:

- Used the funds mix and rate performance of its regional competitors to establish more aggressive funds management benchmarks;

- Used the operating cost management policies of the large national bank to improve its own sales/delivery and operations functions;

- Determined that funds and operations cost management were more powerful "profit levers" than regional and/or new product growth;

- Placed greater emphasis on profit objectives, rather than focusing exclusively on growth objectives

Summary: Examples of Cost Benchmarking Across the Entire Chain

The three examples above illustrate how complete cost chain benchmarking can yield significant insights about how to change the strategy, structure, and profitability of a business. Unlike single function benchmarking which focuses on a given function (see examples in the following chapter) and goes into greater analytic depth, full cost chain benchmarking attempts to provide a broad picture of a firm's overall performance and highlights the key strategic decisions that must be made. Used in tandem, entire cost chain benchmarking and in-depth benchmarking of selected functions can be the basis for dramatic performance improvements.

Chapter 9

Examples of Cost Benchmarking for Individual Functions

The three examples in this chapter provide a simplified overview of typical cost benchmarking analyses for individual functions. The company in the first example used benchmarking to set new sales targets and strategies; the second identified a manufacturing strategy appropriate to changes in the industry's structure; and a third company found ways to bring its management information systems up to par.

Example: Data Technology Salesforce Benchmarking

A large U.S. manufacturer of technology hardware (Company A in the charts below) was concerned with the overall cost and productivity of its salesforce. In order to establish externally based cost and productivity targets, the company benchmarked itself against five key competitors. The objective was to compare Company A's:

- Salesforce expenditures as a percent of total revenues;

- Productivity of its average direct sales rep;

- Salesforce compensation and incentive structure;

- Critical sales management policies which affect cost and productivity.

Through this analysis, Company A hoped to identify areas where it could improve its performance.

Analysis

In the chart below, Company A developed an estimate of its direct sales costs versus those of each of the competitors. The critical benchmarks used in the analysis were average revenues generated per rep (a productivity measure), yearly compensation per rep, the company benefits rate, and a "ballpark" estimate of direct travel expenses per sales rep. Based on these benchmarks, an estimate of total direct sales costs was generated:

Total Direct Sales Cost Travel As % of Revenues	=	Compensation x (1 + Benefits Rate) + Revenues per Rep

DIRECT SALES COST BENCHMARKS

BENCHMARK / COMPANY	REVENUES PER REP	TOTAL COMPENSATION (Salary +Bonus)	BENEFIT RATE	TRAVEL, OTHER DIRECT EXPENSES*	ESTIMATED DIRECT SALES COST*
A (US)	$ 930K	$35K	29%	1.2%	6.1%
B	$ 850K	$32K	27%	1.3%	6.1%
C	$ 970K	$44K	29%	1.1%	7.0%
D	$1,150K	$37K	24%	1.0%	5.0%
E	$1,000K	$29K	22%	1.1%	4.6%
F	$ 780K	$35K	30%	1.2%	7.0%

*As percent of revenues.

Based on this analysis, Company A determined that Competitors D and E had a lower estimated cost of sale and more productive sales reps. To understand why this was so, Company A looked next at management policies affecting sales productivity.

The next chart focuses on a few of these management policy benchmarks. Competitor D's salesforce strategy is driven by offering the sales reps the incentive of a significant commission/bonus as a percent of total compensation (30%) and by giving them a higher level of sales support (1.5 support personnel for every rep). Alternatively, Competitor E achieves its high productivity and low cost by offering the highest level of sales support (1.8:1), reducing sales management investment to the lowest levels, and focusing their sales reps on fewer accounts. These strategies prompted an internal "rethinking" of Company A's salesforce management policies and targets.

FACTORS IMPACTING SALES REP PRODUCTIVITY

	ESTIMATED DIRECT SALES COST*	AVERAGE ACCOUNTS PER SALES PERSON	COMMISSION/ BONUS AS A % OF TOTAL PAY	SALES SUPPORT PERSONNEL PER REP	SALES REPS PER MANAGER
A (U.S.)	6.1%	60	10%	1:1	6:1
B	6.1%	70-80	10%	1.5:1	5:1
C	7.0%	70	10%	1.2:1	6:1
D	5.0%	50	30%	1.5:1	5:1
E	4.6%	25-30	0%	1.8:1	8:1
F	7.2%	40-60	0%	8:1	4:1

*As percent of revenues.

Results

Based on these and several other salesforce benchmarks, Company A decided to make several changes, including:

- Setting higher sales rep revenue targets;

- Offering greater incentive, compensation for achieving the higher targets;

- Providing more sales support personnel to take away administrative tasks from the direct salesforce and allow them to concentrate on making sales calls.

Within nine months, Company A's sales productivity was up almost 15% and sales costs as a percent of revenues had declined significantly.

Example: Manufacturing Benchmarking

Manufacturing benchmarking analyses can take several forms. Some companies have attempted to benchmark competitors' manufacturing costs in as much detail as possible; while these efforts have been successful, they require a significant level of resources to complete. For firms that are not willing or able to make a major commitment of resources, it is sometimes necessary to narrow the scope of a manufacturing benchmarking project in order to focus on the critical factors impacting overall manufacturing cost and performance.

In the example below, an electronics manufacturer recognized the difficulty of benchmarking manufacturing cost for a product with over 200 components. As a result, the company focused on the competitors' assembly operations within manufacturing and developed some broad yet insightful benchmarks to determine its own competitive position. Competitive manufacturing strengths and weaknesses were apparent at the conclusion of this analysis and were used to determine future manufacturing strategy.

Data Systems, a major player in the electronics industry, had recently entered the market for "mobile medical devices," ranging from implantable devices, to drug delivery devices that monitor health and the related biometrics of an individual for specific diseases. (Both the actual segment of the market and the company have been disguised.) While the company had less than 2% share of this rapidly growing market, it was considering a major capital investment in plant and equipment to become a market leader. The market was currently dominated by two mid-size companies, Custom Electronics and Innovation Technology. In addition, Data Systems' largest competitor, National Electronics, had recently entered and captured a 9% share.

In order to develop a winning manufacturing strategy, Data Systems determined that it needed to benchmark the manufacturing capabilities of the three most successful players in the market. The primary goal of the benchmarking effort was to establish the appropriate level of plant automation that Data Systems would need to establish a long-term competitive advantage. The critical issue was how to manage the apparent trade-off between automating to achieve long production runs and low cost, and the need to incorporate line flexibility for product customization.

Analysis

To meet these objectives and better understand the manufacturing strengths and weaknesses of its competitors, Data Systems set up three categories of benchmarks:

- Overall market and manufacturing strategy benchmarks;

- Labor cost and productivity benchmarks;

- Non-labor cost benchmarks.

The first chart below compares the markedly different strategies of each of the three competitors. Custom Electronics, the current market leader and "darling" of Wall Street analysts, had developed marketing and manufacturing strategies targeted at devices serving specific high cost disease states. Its ability to customize products for very special needs and to reduce new product, development cycles to under eighteen months were the clear reasons for the "company's success in the early stages of market development. Innovation Technology, on the other hand, had decided to move away from customization and to begin to standardize its product line; as a result, it had recently invested in capital equipment which reduced the need for direct labor. Finally, National Electronics had recently entered the market with a strong bias toward high volume, highly automated production, but its plant was currently believed to be at low utilization levels.

OVERVIEW OF "MOBILE MEDICAL DEVICE" COMPETITORS' MARKET POSITION & STRATEGY

COMPANY / BENCHMARK	CUSTOM ELECTRONICS	INNOVATIVE TECHNOLOGY	NATIONAL ELECTRONICS
UNIT MARKET SHARE	35%	30%	9%
UNITS PRODUCED/MONTH	4,000	3,500	1,000
MARKETING STRATEGY	• OFFER BROAD PRODUCT LINE • BUILD-TO-ORDER, CUSTOMIZE • SELL DIRECT	• NARROW PRODUCT LINE • BUILD-TO-INVENTORY • SELL THROUGH THIRD PARTY	• RECENTLY ENTERED MARKET WITH SINGLE PRODUCT • TARGET EXISTING MARKET SEGMENTS • FOCUS ON GAINING SHARE
MANUFACTURING STRATEGY	• BUY MOST COMPONENTS ON OPEN MARKET • LABOR-INTENSIVE ASSEMBLY • INVESTING IN SOME LIMITED PROPRIETARY TECHNOLOGY	• INCREASINGLY MAKE MORE COMPONENTS IN-HOUSE • INVESTING IN AUTOMATION • LIMITED PROPRIETARY TECHNOLOGY	• SOURCE MOST COMPONENTS FROM IN-HOUSE PLANTS • 90% AUTOMATED ASSEMBLY • PROPRIETARY TECHNOLOGY

To compare the level of automation within each company's plant, Data Systems collected information such as volume of production, labor headcount, and wage rates for each competitor. The next chart summarizes these results and illustrates that while total labor cost per device produced was comparable across all three competitors, there were significant differences in the wage rates and man-hours per unit. Custom Electronics had a very labor-intensive assembly process but managed to reduce overall labor costs by hiring low paid, relatively unskilled workers. Innovation Technology managed to put fewer labor hours into each unit but paid higher wage rates than Custom Electronics.

Finally, National Electronics exhibited the highest wage rates and the lowest labor hours per unit -- as a result of a higher proportion of management in its labor mix.

"MOBILE MEDICAL DEVICE" MANUFACTURING LABOR BENCHMARKS

	Average Units Per Shift	Direct Assembly Laborers			Indirect Laborers			Management/ Supervisor			Total Labor Cost Per Unit
		Headcount Per Shift	Wage/ Hour	Labor $/Unit	Headcount Per Shift	Wage/ Hour	Labor $/Unit	Headcount Per Shift	Wage	Labor $/Unit	
Custom Electronics	0	370	$ 17.00	$ 630	150	$ 17.00	$ 256	75	$ 64K	$ 240	$ 1126
Innovation Technology	2	180	$ 22.00	$ 440	150	$ 22.00	$ 366	60	$ 62K	$ 206	$ 1012
National Electronics	7	54	$ 24.5	$ 392	32	$ 24.5	$ 232	20	$ 74K	$ 218	$ 842

Finally, the next chart includes key non-labor benchmarks. Custom Electronics exhibited low levels of automation and, owing to its build-to-order strategy, high levels of raw materials and work-in-process. Additionally, Custom had some other problems, including a lower product yield and long order-to-ship cycles. Innovation and National, with greater automation and higher inventory turns, benefited from better production quality and an ability to ship product faster.

SELECTED "MOBILE MEDICAL DEVICE" NON-LABOR MANUFACTURING BENCHMARKS

	GROSS PROPERTY, PLANT AND EQUIPMENT PER DIRECT LABORER	INVENTORY	ESTIMATED AUTOMATED HOURS OF ASSEMBLY	PRODUCT YIELD END OF LINE	PRODUCT ORDER-TO-RECEIPT CYCLE
CUSTOM ELECTRONICS	$320K	Turnover 3.3x Mix-Raw Material: 55% W-I-P: 25% Finished Goods: 20%	30%	95%	30-40 DAYS
INNOVATION TECHNOLOGY	$640K	Turnover 3.5x Mix: Raw Material: 30% W-I-P: 20% Finished Goods: 50%	S0%	97%	5-10 DAYS
NATIONAL ELECTRONICS	$780K	Turnover 4.5x Mix: Raw Material: N/A W-I-P: N/A Finished Goods: N/A	80%	98%	15-25 DAYS

Results

Upon completion of a customer survey, Data Systems found that customer needs in the mobile medical device market were changing rapidly. Product customization was becoming less important than product quality, reliability, and availability. In addition, the customer survey found that as the market grew, customer price sensitivity was increasing. By coupling these results with the manufacturing benchmarking analysis, Data Systems concluded that:

• Custom Electronics was not the competitor with the best manufacturing strategy, despite its leading market share;

• Innovation and National had developed a manufacturing strategy that was better suited to a maturing, higher volume mobile medical device market;

• Data Systems should establish its new plant operations targets based primarily on the performance levels and processes of Innovation and National;

• Data Systems should use the manufacturing benchmarking results in its marketing efforts in order to highlight the quality and delivery weaknesses of Custom Electronics.

Example: IT Function Benchmarking

In the example described below, a major European conglomerate benchmarked its information technology (IT) costs and policies versus those of several other foreign competitors.

In late 2013, a large European corporation with multinational operations was facing a major decision concerning how to restructure its internal IT operations. The old structure had been in place for over a decade and was believed by most employees to be too bureaucratic and to offer too few real services to the corporation in terms of delivering detailed, real-time information to senior management, finance, market and sales and manufacturing. A classic struggle developed between one group of managers that wanted to keep IT management centralized at European headquarters and another group of managers that wanted to decentralize and allow each operating unit to decide on its own level and type of IT resources. To establish a third-party view, a benchmarking project was launched to identify four "best-in-class" corporations renowned for IT excellence.

Analysis

A wide range of analysis was conducted, and only a small sample is shown below. The first chart highlights the level of expenditures on IT of each company as a percent of total corporate revenue. The differences were dramatic, with a multi-national, financial services company spending over three times as much as a large Japanese company. Interestingly, those companies spending more in this area perceived the role of IT to be strategically critical to the corporation; that is, they viewed the function as an important means through which to develop competitive advantage. Conversely, those companies spending less viewed the function as only a necessary support to the rest of the corporation.

In addition, the analysis showed that at least two companies actually ran the IT function as a profit center within the corporation. For these companies, the IT department fully charged internal users for all services as if it were an outside supplier.

IT FUNCTION OVERALL MANAGEMENT BENCHMARKS

	U.S. SEMI-CONDUCTOR MANUFACT-URER	U.S. BASED MULTINATIONAL DEFENSE CONTRACTOR	FINANCIAL SERVICE COMPANY	JAPANESE ELECTRONICS CONGLOMERATE	EUROPEAN ELECTRONICS CONGLOMERATE
IT EXPENDITURES AS PERCENT OF REVENUES	5.5%	3.3%	6.7%	2.1%	3.0%
ROLE OF IT FUNCTION	STRATEGIC	STRATEGIC	STRATEGIC	SUPPORT	SUPPORT
LEVEL OF CENTRALIZATION	DIVISION	GROUP	PRODUCT -- EACH PRODUCT AREA DESIGNS OWN SYSTEMS	REGIONAL DIVISION	CORPORATE
FINANCIAL VIEW OF IT FUNCTION	COST CENTER	PROFIT CENTER	PROFIT CENTER	COST CENTER	COST CENTER

Coupled with more in-depth analysis, these insights led the European managers to focus on a number of questions:

• What role should IT play in the corporation: support or strategic?

• Based on the defined role of the different IT services, at what level in the organization should control be placed so as to minimize cost yet maximize the value offered by the function

• How should the cost of the IT expenditures be recovered from a corporate budget pool or through charging each individual business unit for each service?

A second part of the benchmarking analysis (see chart below) focused on the particular issue of establishing internal private data and voice networks to link the numerous facilities of the corporation worldwide. The European company compared the number of networks each "best-in-class" competitor had put in place and evaluated the level of sophistication and breadth of applications for each network. Again, some companies had built extensive, centralized, worldwide networks while others had relied on numerous separate networks dedicated to a particular geographic area or line of business. These facts pointed to a number of major issues that the European company had to resolve before implementing a new IT strategy.

IT FUNCTION OVERALL MANAGEMENT BENCHMARKS

	U.S. SEMI-CONDUCTOR MANUFACTURER	U.S. BASED MULTI-NATIONAL DEFENSE CONTRACTOR	FINANCIAL SERVICE COMPANY	JAPANESE ELECTRONICS CONGLOMER-ATE	EUROPEAN ELECTRONICS CONGLOMER-ATE
NUMBER OF PRIVATE TELECOM NETWORKS	ONE CORPORATE-WIDE SYSTEM	ONE CORPORATE-WIDE SYSTEM	FIFTY: EACH PRODUCT HAS OWN NETWORK	10-15 SEPARATE NETWORKS FOR EACH REGION	TWO (BOTH IN EUROPE)
NETWORK SOPHISTICA-TION	HIGH	MODERATE	HIGH	LOW	MODERATE
DECREE OF VOICE/DATA INTEGRATION	HIGH	LOW	LOW	MODERATE	LOW
FUNCTIONS USING NETWORK	ALL - FINANCE - SALES - MARKET- ING - MANU-FACTUR-ING - R & D	PRIMARILY FINANCE, R & D AND MANUFACT-URING	PRIMARILY TRANSACT-IONS PROCESS-ING	FINANCE, MARKETING	FINANCE

Results

At the conclusion of the benchmarking project, the European conglomerate decided that:

- The company would be ill-advised to maintain its bureaucratic and relatively ineffective centralized control over IT;

- Decentralization of IT expenditures would be encouraged so that each operating unit could decide for itself what level of IT support it needed to successfully compete;

- A corporate-level committee would be established to set broad policies that would ensure systems compatibility and interoperability of IT and telecommunications across geographic and business boundaries.

Summary: Single Function Benchmarking Examples

In each of the examples cited above, the results of the benchmarking process established objective reference points against which the company's operations could be compared, and through which critical problem areas could be identified. In each of the examples, the "gap" between one's own business and the best-in-class competitors was identified, externally-based operating targets were established, and programs were put in place to improve the business' operating position. The managers who used these benchmarking results found that better and faster decisions were made and that the business' competitive positions were markedly improved.

Chapter 10

Benchmarking Differentiation

Differentiation allows competitors to earn higher prices and/or gain greater market share. Benchmarking efforts aimed at understanding how companies achieve differentiation can be just as critical as cost benchmarking for improving your organization's competitive position and profitability.

There are essentially four ways to differentiate your offering:

- Provide superior product features;

- Provide superior product quality;

- Offer higher levels of customer service;

- Develop a superior brand image.

Most firms attempt to differentiate their offerings on at least two of these four dimensions. To do so successfully, you must first establish a set of standards against which to measure your product's differentiation. Benchmarking of differentiation requires information on competitors and, in many cases, customers' input on purchasing criteria and on how they rate the various suppliers.

Benchmarking of each of the four types of differentiation is described as follows.

Product Features Benchmarking

One way of comparing one's product to that of the competition is by analyzing relative product features. For example, in the case of mobile phones, typical product features would include:

- Screen size

- SD card slot

- SG vs 4G

- Style

- Color options

- Battery life

- Price point

- Apps library

Companies can easily determine the set of features a competitor is offering on its phones and can compare to one's own offering to determine key differences.

However, most feature comparisons are not as simple as the mobile phone example. First, many products are technologically more complex and can have hundreds of distinct, separate features. Benchmarking a company's points of differentiation in these cases can be complex. Secondly, it is often unclear whether a superior product feature really translates into real differentiation as perceived by the customer. For example, in the early 1980's, AT&T developed a facsimile machine that transmitted in multiple colors. While this was a technological breakthrough, there were very few customers who felt the need to use a color facsimile machine. As a result, this feature did not offer AT&T any significant differentiation at the time.

There are three steps for benchmarking product features versus competitors. They are:

- Determine the most important set of features to the customer. In some cases you will find that what is important to one customer group is not the same as what is important to another. In these cases, it may be necessary to identify the most important product features for each customer segment.

- Compare your product's features to those of the competitors.

- Determine your major areas of strength and weakness, keeping in mind the customers' feature preferences and priorities. The key is make sure your product includes those features which are most important to the customer. The goal is not to include all possible features, but rather to incorporate only those features that the customer is willing to pay for.

A variation on this analysis is comparison of the range of <u>feature options</u> offered to the customer. The Japanese auto companies successfully penetrated the U.S. auto market despite offering a limited number of option packages. U.S. manufacturers raised their manufacturing cost by thousands of dollars per car by offering much greater variety. The U.S. companies have learned belatedly that for many customers, the added value of that variety was not worth the underlying cost.

Product Quality Benchmarking

When benchmarking was implemented at Xerox in the late 1970s, one of its original purposes was to improve product quality. Since then, there has been a dramatic increase in the emphasis on quality improvement among U.S. corporations, and benchmarking has been one important element of those efforts.

In benchmarking quality against the "best-in-class," it is critical to understand not only the levels of quality achieved but also the management methods used to achieve them. While the field of measuring and benchmarking product quality is still developing, several quality benchmarking measures are typically considered:

- Production yields (percentage of units determined to be below standard after manufacture)

- Rework rates (percentage of products quality corrected after manufacture)

- Warranty expense/repair costs

- Mean time between product failures ("reliability")

- Mean time to repair ("serviceability")

- Quality methods such as worker participation, quality controls and innovative manufacturing processes

Quality benchmarking is also based on customer input. Companies may survey customers' perceptions of the quality of competing products in order to supplement the data listed above. One equipment manufacturer was convinced that its product quality was superior based on strenuous engineering tests, only to find that customers didn't perform those tests and considered the competitor's product quality to be superior based on other criteria.

Service Benchmarks

A comparison of your product's features and quality levels to those of the competition does not comprise a full differentiation benchmarking effort. As many corporations are learning, a business can often gain market share or earn higher prices without changing the product. Service has become a critical area in which companies can successfully differentiate themselves and thus outperform the competition.

Service refers to the process of interacting with the customer. Service can range from a salesperson's call on the customer, to the service technician who repairs a machine on-site, to the customer service representative who answers the phone when the customer calls. Typical benchmarks of service differentiation include:

- Hours of availability of personnel

- Response time

- Repair time

- Measures of speed of delivery, such as "fill rate"

- Order-to-receipt cycle time

- Quality of the personnel interacting with the customer, *e.g.,* level of experience and nature of expertise

- Order entry systems, *e.g.,* ability to order products quickly via telephone or computer

- Availability of training and informal "consulting" for the customer

- Customer complaint volume

As product advantages become harder and harder to maintain in many industries, benchmarking of services as a way to achieve differentiation is becoming increasingly important.

Benchmarking Image

Finally, a vendor's image can have a significant effect on its ability to differentiate its offering. It is useful to benchmark image both by measuring customers' reactions and by understanding how the competition invests in building its image.

Customer inputs include:

- Awareness levels

- Positive (or negative) association with various vendors

- Positive (or negative) association with specific aspects of the various vendors' image (*e.g.,* quality, responsiveness, integrity, etc.)

Competitive inputs include:

- Level of advertising

- Media selected for advertising

- Message of advertising

- Promotions

- Participation in trade shows

- Public relations efforts

- Actions aimed at influencing opinion leaders

The Trade-Off: Differentiation vs. Cost

As with product features, the goal is not to provide the most possible quality, service, and image, but rather only those aspects of differentiation for which the customer is willing to pay. (Willingness to pay [WTP] is the greatest sum a person or entity is prepared to pay for a product or service. It should be noted that in many platform type businesses such as Facebook, We Chat, etc. for which an 'app' has been developed the product or service is essentially free). Consciously addressing the trade-off between differentiation and cost is a crucial part of the benchmarking process.

There are a variety of ways to assess that trade-off, ranging from purely subjective judgments to statistical sampling techniques to in-depth customer research. However, while quantitative methods can provide valuable input, in the end management must make a judgment call to determine the appropriate level of differentiation.

Although the benchmarking of differentiation will not "give you the answer" (*i.e.,* tell you with certainty how much differentiation the customer is willing to pay for), it will enable you to identify and focus on competitive differences and to address explicitly the cost/differentiation trade-off. That is the primary value of differentiation benchmarking, for managers who analyze competitive differentiation explicitly and with good competitive data will almost always come to a better decision than those who do not.

Chapter 11

Examples of Benchmarking Differentiation

Example: Videoconference Differentiation Benchmarking

With the rapid growth of high speed telecommunications in the 1980s and 1990s, videoconferencing services began to be launched by third party vendors. As the speed and bandwidth of telecommunication services improved, so did these videoconferencing services and, in 2014, a major Fortune 100 company decided to re-evaluate its videoconferencing services for both internal and external communication, especially as the right service could potentially cut down expensive and time consuming executive travel between the company's many sites around the world. It was also essential that any service or services that were supported centrally by the corporate IT department had to meet the security standards of inter-office communication as virtually free videoconference via the Internet with services such as Skype had become available, but had little or no encryption and did not meet corporate standards.

Analysis

To resolve the problem, IT leadership decided to benchmark their videoconferencing services against those used by three "best-in-class" companies known to have significant global corporate videoconferencing services. While none of these companies were in the exact same industry, the internal function of providing videoconferencing to executives was believed to be similar across all four. The first step in the process was to compare the features and capabilities of the various systems being used by all target companies. The chart below compares fourteen critical features across each of the four companies. Product W was offered by one of the major global IT vendors. In developing this service, it had had a long history of innovation and adding features. By 2010, its offering included *180 degree* rap around screens and mobile options, as well as the highest level of encryption, security and central management of the service. However, Product W was also costing its users significantly more than the other companies' videoconferencing services, some which were made up of multiple vendors and could not be interconnected.

VIDEOCONFERENCING SERVICE FEATURE COMPARISON CHART

FEATURE	PRODUCT			
	W	X	Y	Z
VIDEOCONFERENCING SERVICES				
-- SEND / RECEIVE	X	X	X	X
-- STORE / FILE	X	X	X	X
-- MESSAGING	X	X	X	X
LINKED TO CORPORATE CALENDARS	X	X	X	
LINKED TO CLOUD-BASED STORAGE	X	X		
PHONE DIRECTORY				
GLOBAL CONNECTIVITY	X	LIMITED	LIMITED	LIMITED
ACCESSABLE FROM DECKTOPS AND MOBILE	X	X	X	
FULL SESSION ENCRIPTION ON ALL HARDWARE, WIFI AND VOIP	X	LIMITED	LIMITED	LIMITED
CUSTOM VIDEO ROOMS	X			
ZERO RE-SET TIME	X			
CENTRALLY MANAGED ARCHITECTURE	X	X	X	
NUMBER OF USERS	30,000	5,000	15.000	23,000
AVERAGE SESSIONS / USER / MONTH	4.2	2.8	3.2	2.2
AVERAGE COST / HOUR	$500	$100	$50	$150

Discussions with IT managers at the other companies revealed that the services used varied by when they were installed by the vendors. With the constant improvement in telecommunications speed, band width and wide-screen hardware, options were available on later installations that were not available on earlier. One of the earlier issues with videoconferencing was the time lapse and synchronization of video and sound between parties in remote locations, especially when they were on different continents. Minimizing these effects made a major difference to the quality of the services and the satisfaction of users. It was clear that there was a direct correlation between usage and these features, customer satisfaction and, in turn, to reductions in white-collar executive travel and cost savings.

To compare each services relative position, analysts created the two "trade-off" charts in the illustration below. The analysis showed that there was a direct correlation between customer satisfaction and system costs and functionality. A separate market research exercise was carried to estimate the potential travel savings against the customer satisfaction of the videoconference systems, which allowed the firm to estimate the optimal service for potential travel savings.

VIDEOCONFERENCING COST AND FUNCTIONALITY VS. CUSTOMER SATIFACTION TRADE-OFFS

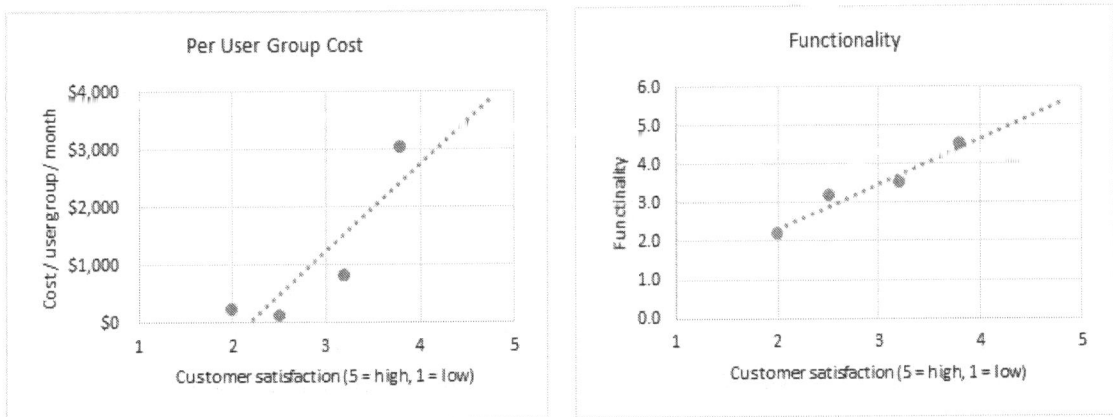

To relate these trade-offs of the potential saving in travel costs for the firm, a survey was taken of managers who regular travel to get their opinion of the reduction in travel with different levels of videoconferencing functionality. Using the above trade-off charts, this work was converted to comparing total travel costs to customer satisfaction of videoconferencing services and these

TOTAL ANNUAL COSTS OF VIDEOCONFERENCING VS TOTAL POTENTIAL MANAGEMENT TRAVEL COSTS

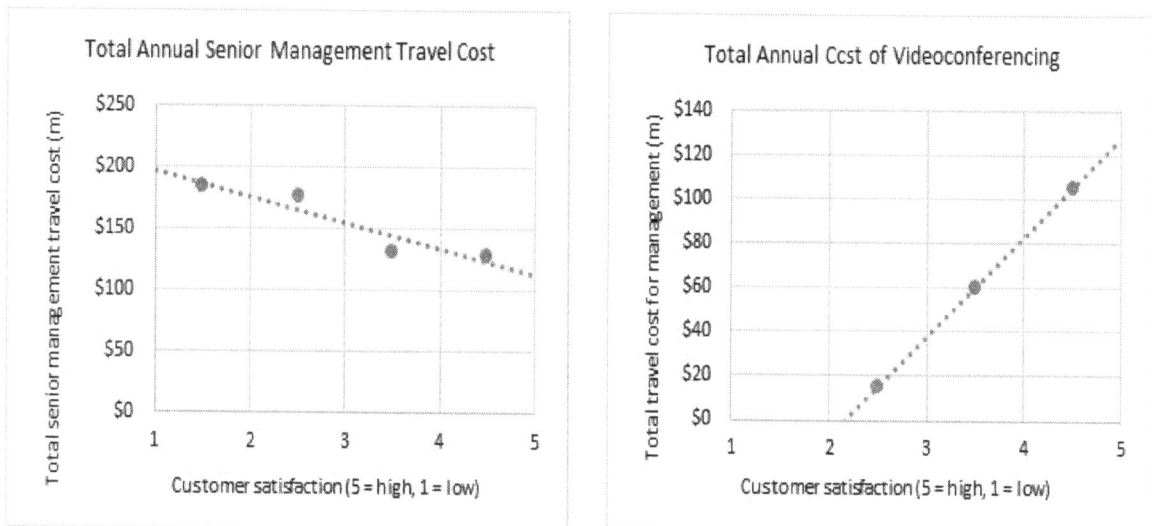

Results

The results of this benchmarking analysis can be summarized as follows:

- With the current relationships between functionality, customer satisfaction and cost, the annual extra cost of using a high functionality videoconferencing service was not offset by a near equal saving in estimated travel cost, implying that the firm should not invest in most expensive service purely on the basis of travel cost savings

- However, this analysis also showed was that if the cost of high functionality systems decreased due to technology advantages, the cost saving from travel could more than cover the cost of videoconferencing

The above example shows not only how product differentiation can affect costs, but also how a reduction of a product or service functionality can be as important as increasing its capabilities. It also shows that any exercise involving technology, must also consider the dynamics of technology innovation and how this is likely to impact future costs and savings. The next two examples show how two companies benchmarked differentiation and determined that they needed to "increase costs" and add capabilities and services to their offering.

Example: Parts Aftermarket Support Benchmarking

In one U.S. industry, manufacturers must continually address a key trade-off: should they make profits on aftermarket parts sales or sacrifice profits by providing low-cost parts and high levels of customer service? This latter strategy would hopefully pay off in the form of increased brand loyalty and, in the long-run, greater market share.

To learn how various manufacturers make this trade-off, one U.S. company (Competitor A) completed a detailed benchmarking of parts distribution profitability and performance among seven leading competitors. Four broad areas of parts operations performance were benchmarked (see chart below):

```
                    ┌─────────────────────┐
                    │  PARTS OPERATIONS   │
                    │     BENCHMARKS      │
                    └─────────────────────┘
```

CUSTOMER SATISFACTION	DEALER SUPPORT	PARTS AVAILABILITY	SALES AND PROFIT
• RESULTS OF END-USER SURVEY	• DISTRICT MANAGERS AND ZONE OFFICE SUPPORT • MERCHANDISING PROGRAMS • PRODCUT PROMOTION AND DEVELOPMENT • ADVERTISING PROGRAMS	• FILL RATE • PARTS AVAILABILITY • CUSTOMER RETENTION RATE	• SALES PRODUCTIVITY • PARTS MARGINS • INVENTORY TURNOVER • RETURN ON INVENTORY

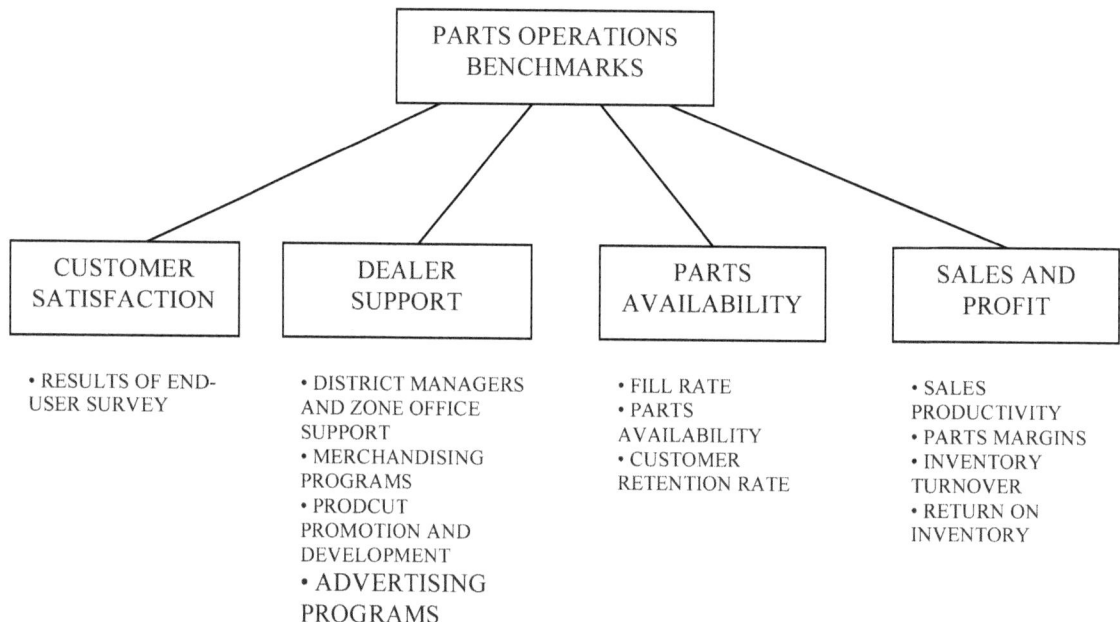

- End-Use Customer Satisfaction with Dealer Parts and Repair

  -- data was collected from customer surveys;

- Dealer Parts Support Levels

  -- amount of resources devoted to serving dealers' parts businesses;

- Parts Availability

  -- level of product availability to both dealers and customers;

- Parts Operations Profitability.

The seven companies to be benchmarked included the three largest U.S. manufacturers, the three largest Japanese manufacturers, and one European manufacturer. Data for each of these companies was collected from published sources and from interviews with dealers, customers, and parts distributors. The results indicated that the expected "trade-off" between parts operations profitability and customer satisfaction was not necessarily a given -- the Japanese manufacturers offered high parts service levels <u>and</u> simultaneously achieved good parts profitability.

Analysis

The overall ranking of each manufacturer is displayed in the chart below. Company A had the highest parts profitability of any competitor, but ranked lowest in terms of customer satisfaction, next to lowest for parts availability, and only "average" in terms of dealer support levels. On the other hand, Japan Company D consistently ranked in the top half in each service category while also maintaining the second highest profitability as measured by "return on inventory." The Japanese company appeared to be the "best-in-class" company in terms of overall parts distribution.

OVERALL RANKING OF PARTS OPERATIONS

	CUSTOMER SATISFACTION LEVEL: SURVEY RESULTS	DEALER SUPPORT	PARTS AVAILABILITY	PROFITABILITY	
				OPERATING MARGINS	RETURN ON INVENTORY
HIGHEST	EUROPE G	JAPAN D	EUROPE G	U.S. A	U.S. A
	JAPAN F	U.S. B	JAPAN F	U.S. B	JAPAN D
	JAPAN D	JAPAN F	JAPAN D	U.S. C	JAPAN F
	JAPAN E	U.S. A	JAPAN E	JAPAN D	JAPAN E
	U.S. B	JAPAN E	U.S. B	JAPAN E	U.S. B
LOWEST	U.S. C	U.S. C	U.S. A	JAPAN F	U.S. C
	U.S. A	EUROPE G	U.S. C	EUROPE G	EUROPE G

173

Some of the detail behind these rankings is highlighted in the next two charts. The first chart highlights the companies' comparative positions in parts availability (percent of parts available at dealer when customer walks in) and fill rate (percent of parts orders filled within 24 hours). As the data show, the foreign companies excel at these functions relative to their U.S. counterparts. The second chart breaks down parts profitability into gross parts margin, parts inventory turnover (revenues divided by average parts inventory), and "return on inventory" (gross margin divided by average inventory levels). The Japanese companies have lower gross margins. However, they make up for low margins by having higher inventory turnover and therefore have comparable overall profitability.

BENCHMARKING PARTS AVAILABILITY AND FILL RATE

	PARTS AVAILABILITY	FILL RATE
U.S. A	64%	82%
U.S. B	65%	85%
U.S. C	61%	84%
JAPAN D	75%	95%
JAPAN E	69%	90%
JAPAN F	80%	94%

EUROPE G	84%	96%

PARTS PROFITABILITY COMPARISON

	U.S. MANUFACTURERS			JAPANESE MANUFACTURERS			EUROPEAN MANUFACTURERS
	A	B	C	D	E	F	G
PARTS MARGIN	40%	38%	36%	20%	25%	25%	16%
INVENTORY TURNOVER (Warehouse & Dealer)	1.18	0.95	.90	2.32	1.62	1.85	.93
RETURN ON TOTAL SYSTEM INVENTORY*	47%	36%	32%	46%	41%	46%	15%

* Parts Margin x Inventory Turnover.

Results

In sum, U.S. Competitor A "trades off" profits and customer satisfaction levels -- profits are high, but customer and dealer support suffers. However, the Japanese have achieved good profitability and dealer/customer satisfaction levels. As a result of this analysis, managers at Company A:

• Increased dealer support levels with the goal of becoming #1 in dealer support;

• Established more ambitious parts availability, fill rate, and inventory turnover targets based on their competitors' performance levels;

175

- Began monitoring customer satisfaction levels with the goal of improving its satisfaction ranking and gaining greater brand loyalty.

Example: Electrical Equipment Service Benchmarking

Company B, the number two player in a commercial electrical equipment market, recently found itself losing market share and realizing lower price levels than its competition. In particular, the market leader (Company A) was earning a 10%-15% higher price on comparable products and was maintaining its strong market share (above 60%). Company C, a small upstart, was gaining market share in particular regions of the country and was believed to be earning a slight (2%-5%) price premium.

According to customer surveys, Company B's disadvantage was largely due to a much lower level of service, in particular the level of technical support offered to the architects and contractors installing the systems. In addition, Company B's distributors were complaining about the low level of service they were receiving compared to the service Company A provided for its distributors. To verify the problem and determine the source of these differences, a service benchmarking study was conducted.

Analysis

The first part of the study focused on technical support levels being offered to the architects and building contractors. As summarized in the chart below, the key finding was that Companies A and C were both investing significantly higher resources toward the technical support function, both in terms of headcount and compensation of technical service reps.

ELECTRICAL EQUIPMENT DIFFERENTIATION BENCHMARKS

BENCHMARK / COMPANY	MARKET SHARE	SHARE TREND	MARKET PRICE PREMIUM	TECHNICAL SUPPORT COST AS % REVENUES	TECHNICAL REPS/ $100MM REVENUE	TECHNICAL REP COMPENSATION
COMPANY A	63%	FLAT	+10-15%	4.1%	36	$38K
COMPANY B	22%	LOSING	-	< 1	4	$31K
COMPANY C	14%	GAINING	+2-+25%	2.2%	12	$48K

The result was that the competitors' tech service reps were making more frequent contact with the real decision-makers -- the architects and engineers designing buildings and specifying the type of system to be installed. Company B managers attributed a large part of the market share loss and price erosion to this large competitive disadvantage.

In addition, Company B benchmarked the level of service it was currently offering its distributors relative to the service provided by its competitors. The chart below illustrates that while the company was somewhat competitive with Company C, Company A was investing heavily in dealer support. While Company B knew it did not have the resources to completely match the market leader, it determined that it must somehow narrow the service gap between itself and the competition.

BENCHMARKS OF SERVICES OFFERED DISTRIBUTORS

	COMPANY A	COMPANY B	COMPANY C
NATIONAL ADVERTISING SUPPORT	$5MM / YEAR	NO	<$500,000
CO-OP ADVERTISING	YES	YES	NO
TRAINING	EXTENSIVE	LIMITED	NO
WARRANTY COVERAGE	YES	YES (Parts only)	YES
INVENTORY CARRYING (Floor plans)	6 MONTHS AT DISTRIBUTOR SITE	2 MONTHS	2 MONTHS
AUTOMATIC ORDER ENTRY	TO BE INTRODUCED IN 6 MONTHS	NO	NO

Results

The benchmarking process identified several areas where Company B's service levels were deficient relative to the competition. As a result of the analysis, Company B:

- Increased its number of technical support reps and increased the salary scale. This gave the company greater support coverage and allowed them to hire more skilled service reps.

- Revamped its dealer support programs to provide stronger incentives to its dealers to carry and move the Company B product.

After a period of twelve months, Company B had reversed its market share decline and had begun to earn a slight price premium over its smaller competitor. Company B attributed its performance turnaround to the differentiation benchmarking effort.

Chapter 12

Operational Benchmarking: How Detailed?

Operational benchmarking efforts -- whether focused on cost or differentiation -- can be conducted at different levels of detail. Although any level of detail is possible, most operational benchmarking analyses fall into either of two categories:

- Key factors analysis;

- In-depth analysis.

Key factors analysis is represented by the nine examples included in Chapters 8, 9, and 11. Data is gathered for a finite number of key variables. For example, for cost benchmarking, data is gathered for six to twelve components of the cost chain, with three to five cost drivers for each category. The analysis is typically completed in two to three months.

The vast majority of operational benchmarking analyses fall into this category. These efforts can be extremely valuable because, for a relatively small amount of effort, some powerful conclusions can be reached about how to reduce one's own cost or to improve differentiation.

However, key factors analysis clearly has its limitations. While the analysis identifies major areas where you are at a competitive disadvantage, as well as the underlying reasons, there is sometimes detailed tactical or "implementation" analysis which remains to be done after a key factors analysis is completed.

The second type of operational benchmarking, in-depth analysis, is far more detailed. Many dozens or even hundreds of individuals typically get involved, and the effort can take years and cost millions of dollars. Obviously, not everyone can afford to do this type of benchmarking, but if there is top management support and the dollars are available, the results can be dramatic. Two companies that have taken this approach are Xerox and Ford, and their experience is described in the following chapter.

The approach to be selected is clearly a function of time and money available and what you are trying to accomplish. Unless there is strong top management support and major resources available, the key factors analysis is the correct approach and usually yields insights and cost savings worth many times the effort expended.

Chapter 13

An Example of In-depth Analysis

The Lesson from Tesla

One would think that an auto company preparing to launch a $40,000 car in late 2017 or so would benchmark its efforts against other manufacturers of similarly priced cars—and there are plenty to choose from in that price category. Tesla, however, took what Robert Frost called "the road less traveled by." It benchmarked its efforts against a practice that Lamborghini, Ferrari, and other top-end luxury sports cars have used for years: pay a deposit and then stand in line for eventual delivery of your car. (Interestingly, private jet manufacturers and luxury yacht builders have also used this approach for decades.)

The "benchmarking question" (what Tesla needed to know from its targeted companies) was simply this: how does a company extract $1000 from a potential customer based solely on artist sketches and the chassis of an earlier model Tesla? (No prototype of the M 3 was ready for public display.) Tesla learned immediately that mail campaigns for this amount of money just don't work, at least not in the volume that Tesla desired as a financial base for manufacturing the M 3.

The best advice it received from its substantial benchmarking research was "go to the customer where he or she lives—at the mall." Tesla took a risk—a substantial one, in hindsight—by leasing high-visibility, expensive mall space in major cities across the U.S. and in selected foreign cities to chat up the virtues of the M 3 (without showing it to customers) and guarantee them a place in line for a "reserve payment" of $1000. To ease the transaction, Tesla promised each potential customer that they could get their $1000 back up to one week before their car was headed down the assembly line.

Tesla apparently had no "Plan B" if this approach failed. It had signed year-long leases in many cases in major malls. It had hired a staff of seasoned car salesmen to staff the showrooms (although little was really being shown). In the annals of auto sales, this gambit was perhaps one of the biggest roll of the dice ever taken by a car company, especially one that was relatively new to playing field.

But it worked, surpassing even Tesla's most optimistic forecasts. Their benchmarking from upscale car, jet, and yacht companies had steered them right: customers who perceive an opportunity to "stand in line" ahead of their neighbors will do so if a) the eventual product is desirable, as the M 3 certainly is, and b) the "reserve price" for the waiting line is within their means. $1000 seemed about right to Tesla, and obviously seemed acceptable to potential customers. As this book goes to press, almost 500,000 have ponied up $1000 for the right to buy an M 3 at no particular discount when it finally arrives on the market. In round figures, that's $500,000,000 *interest-free* money that Tesla could put immediately to work building its enormous battery and assembly plant in Nevada (the largest "footprint" of any single building ever constructed on the planet) and regular, glossy communications with its cadre of $1000 customers, most of whom will follow through and actually purchase the M 3 when it comes to market.

For our purposes, it is the power of benchmarking that is crucial here. Tesla leaders did not merely convene in a board room and come up with a bright idea. Instead, they asked the hard question: has this risky approach ever worked before for companies selling the right to buy a highly desirable item at a future date yet to be determined. The answer came back, "Yes." The company took the risk and apparently has won handsomely.

Further examples of the techniques and benefits of benchmarking can be found in Appendix A (Ford's Taurus and Sable), Appendix B (Benchmarking at Xerox), and Appendix C (Decisions about Internal Customer Call Centers).

Chapter 14

Other Applications of Operational Benchmarking

Once your company has achieved "best-in-class" status through benchmarking, you can apply the same techniques to other applications.

One large consumer products company has significantly improved its own cost position and differentiation through its benchmarking efforts. It is now focusing on encouraging each of its major suppliers to benchmark themselves against the competition.

In doing so, it has instructed each supplier to demonstrate how it will achieve "world class" costs, technology, and delivery schedules. Any supplier not willing to do so will be replaced.

At the other end of the chain, some companies have found they are being hurt by the poor performance of their distributors. In some businesses, downstream distribution (whether one-, two-, or three-tiered) represents as much as 40% to 60% of the total price paid by the end-use customer. If your costs are competitive, but your distributors' costs are not, you may be just as bad off as if your <u>own</u> costs were out of line. There is often a lot to be gained by benchmarking downstream distribution, because it is an area that in many cases has not been studied as closely as your own operations.

Similarly, some component suppliers have benchmarked their customers (*i.e.,* "assemblers") against other assembly competitors to determine the long-term competitive viability of those customers. When the analysis shows that its customers are likely to lose long-term, a component supplier may choose to try to develop relationships with the assemblers who stack up better in terms of the benchmarking analysis.

Finally, benchmarking can be a valuable tool to apply to an acquisitions analysis or program. Benchmarking can identify the competitiveness and value of a potential acquisition, as well as the opportunity for improvement. Companies which have mastered the benchmarking technique typically make acquisition "mistakes" with much lower frequency.

Part IV:

Managing the Benchmarking Process

Chapter 15

The Role of Managing Knowledge in Benchmarking

No company gives its employees rigorous tests each week to get a handle on the total state (in terms of quality and quantity) of knowledge existing within the company at any given point in time. Instead, we tend to rely on observed and anecdotal evidence of employees' knowledge, based on their work product, their contributions at meetings and in written communications, and their record of on-the-job training and seminar participation. In addition, we look upon an employee resume, including college degrees and other certificates, as indications of knowledge available to the organization.

But these measures are hardly sufficient as benchmarks of the quality and quantity of knowledge that can be drawn upon by the company when needed. Take the resume, for example. In hiring a new manager, we have a record (which we hope is true) of his or her *past* knowledge competence, as measured by college tests, papers, and "final exams." The past, however, is just that: the past. Where he or she *is*, in terms of knowledge competence, can be a very different story from where he or she *was* as a university student. Historical knowledge is not contemporary knowledge or predictive knowledge: benchmarking past academic accomplishments of your employees is no guarantee of their present or future abilities to tackle company challenges and opportunities. A company must therefore pay close attention to *atrophy* in the total sum of corporate knowledge.

What Can Happen to Knowledge in Organizations

1. *Knowledge can be born.* What apparently distinguishes *Homo sapiens* from the rest of the animal world is our ability to conceive, store, and manipulate ideas linguistically apart from the stimuli that gave rise to them.

We can think about a name "apples"—make recipes for them, use their visual image for decoration, even name computers after them—without being under the influence of the smell, taste, feel, and appearance of actual apples. We can give birth to ideas as well as manipulate and change them.

Certainly every company desires such intellectual fertility on the part of its employees, particularly its leaders. But what are the circumstances that prove most conducive to the birth of new knowledge in organizations? Which individuals are most adept in their ability to generate new knowledge? What these individuals and not others? How can these individuals be discovered and nurtured? These are questions asked by organizations of all kinds. Companies crave knowledge spawners much as living organisms crave reproductive opportunities and capabilities. In both cases, the motive is the same: survival and maximization of life experience—including business experience.

Knowledge spawners equip their organizations to confront change successfully. For example, rapidly changing global markets can threaten the viability of even the most established businesses, as we have observed recently in the oil business. Companies rely on new knowledge to maintain old markets and extend their business into new fields. These companies' knowledge spawners come up with the biomedical formulae, the algorithm for a faster chip, the alloy for a lighter auto body, or the economic model for a better deployment of resources that allows their organization to thrive while others are failing.

Increasingly, the spawning of knowledge involves a partnership between human cognition and machine-based knowledge. When a pharmaceutical company conducts a complex series of drug tests by means of computer analysis, when a physician makes a diagnosis based primarily on output from an expert cyber system, when an aeronautics corporation designs an aircraft from computer-based flight test data, the question of where requisite knowledge resides for these accomplishments is not easily answered. On one hand, human project designers and data interpreters are certainly important knowledge sources. On the other hand, computers and other systems generate substantial and significant knowledge. While traditionally based on human inputs and management, the artificial intelligence programmed into modern computer systems is increasingly making knowledge a matter of self-generation by artificial intelligence rather than an "import" from a by-standing human, no matter what his or her intellectual pedigree.

Therefore, any plan to manage knowledge in an organization must make provision for both direct human contributions and indirect human knowledge, as mediated and often created by machines empowered to extend and enhance the power of the human mind.

2. Knowledge can die. In terms of sheer quantity, the vast majority of "things known by human beings" die with them. Few of us record even on-thousandth of our knowledge accumulated from our lifetimes. Put in organizational terms, we are individually quite poor at "transition planning" when it comes to passing on our knowledge. Our stores of knowledge go with us to the grave almost entirely whole, leaving each new generation to re-invent a great deal of knowledge (both practical and theoretical) that could have been its birthright.

It could be argued, of course, that most important knowledge achieved during individual human lives gets preserved in the form of books, journal and magazine articles, patents, documentaries, oral histories, and other means. By this logic, the loss of sheer quantity of knowledge through mortality is adequately compensated for by preservation of the *quality* of human knowledge—"the best is saved," in this way of thinking. In effect, we save the tip of the iceberg and therefore do not mourn the loss of the great uninformed and unexamined mass of knowledge beneath the surface. For example, we cling to the works of Mozart (the tip of the musical iceberg) and are hardly aware of what is means to lose the capacity (*i.e,* the genius) to produce such magnificent works.

This is to say that true knowledge management must attend not merely to the totems of knowledge that survive human mortality, but also to the vast "database," the total knowledge-generating skills of a human being such as

Mozart. Too often, we rush to harvest the fruits of knowledge while allowing the tree itself to wither, decay, and ultimately disappear. Knowledge management in organizations involves preserving as much of the "tree"—the root, trunk and branches responsible for the birth of new knowledge—as well as the fruit it produces. Einstein willed his brain to science with just this end in mind. It was his hope that someday the world would discover where his ideas came from, not just what appeared in print.

The death of knowledge for an organization occurs by means other than the mortality of its members. Firms that downsize without making any provision to preserve and extend necessary intellectual capital can find themselves brain dead after terminations and layoffs. After all, knowledge does *not* reside primarily in company manuals and databases, no matter how extensive (and often unused). Instead, company knowledge resides first and foremost within company heads. When "head count" is reduced in a company, inevitably the sum of knowledge within the organization is reduced, sometimes critically so. This happens especially when a firm looks first to its highest paid, longest tenured employees as prime candidates for corporate bloodletting. From a financial management perspective, terminating a few highly-paid employees may be less traumatic than firing many of the rank-and-file employees. but from a knowledge management perspective, cutting off the experienced head from the body of the company may be foolish and expensive surgery indeed.

Knowledge can also die due to paradigm shifts. Aspects of knowledge that were important or sacred for one generation (for example, how to bang dents out of metal auto bodies in the 1980s) may cease to matter for another generation. Understanding human health, as another example, was inconceivable in Western medieval culture apart from the theory of bodily "humors" (behavior-influencing fluids supposedly flowing through the body, including phlegm, choler, and black bile.) Their knowledge of these undocumented substances has become entirely obsolete, even anti-intellectual, because the paradigms we use to understand mental and physical health have changed. Schools now devote little if any time to the medieval humors ("Can Johnny recite the bodily symptoms attributable to black bile?") and most of us would object to the reintroduction of such old paradigms into the modern school curriculum. Just as we have moved away from old, seemingly useless knowledge from the past, later generations may disdain our use of electro-convulsive (ECT) therapy for depression, chemotherapy for cancer, or drugs that impact brain chemistry, such as Prozac or Xanax (the latter being the most prescribed drug in the world).

When paradigm shifts occur, little intellectual effort is spent proving the past wrong. All knowledge resources quickly scurry to the larger and more important task of proving the new paradigm right. When the knowledge paradigm from the past shifts, the knowledge of the past is not "killed" or proven to be wrong. Instead, it is allowed to die from inattention. In this sense, paradigm shifts arise from the focus of new paradigm thinkers to explain the virtues of the new path, not to obsess on what was wrong with the old ways.

Much is lost in such wholesale dismissal of knowledge that was attached to old paradigms in a company. Business organizations too easily find themselves embroiled in perpetual knowledge revolution ("Out with the old! In with the new!") rather than involved in meaningful knowledge growth. True knowledge management within an organization takes the death of previous knowledge seriously and accepts no new paradigm on blind faith. Knowledge management at its best seeks to understand causes for the failing health or death of previous ways of knowing and doing within the company. It salvages what it can from the demise of an old knowledge paradigm.

Finally, knowledge can die from too little or too much exercise. Unexercised knowledge, in the form of rote memorization of facts (such as the periodic table, the capital cities of countries around the world, and so forth) proves difficult for most of us simply because we see the task as useless. Knowledge unattached to purpose is short-lived. Those few among use who manage to become repositories of facts for their own sake are usually seen as social oddity whose quick-recall ability is mildly diverting and quaint. Winners of TV shows such as *Jeopardy* hold great stores of knowledge but are unequipped to write great books, lead social movements, compose symphonies, or further scientific inquiry. Their knowledge is stillborn. It attaches itself to no larger purpose and for that reason falls into insignificance.

Knowledge management in progressive organizations discourages the illusion that the amassing of facts, of and by itself, automatically leads to creative problem-solving or meaningful innovation. The health of a knowledge based in any organization is measured not primarily by its physical size ("how many facts do you know?") but by its agility and muscle tone when put the test of solving organizational problems or seizing company opportunities. The ability on the part of any employee to create and innovate adds far more value to the organization than the ability to recite facts divorced from any purpose.

Curiously, knowledge can die as easily in an organization from too much exercise as too little—that is, from overuse when perpetually attached to a favorite company agenda or traditional purpose. If we are serious about finding a cure for cancer, for example, our researchers must leave room in their methods and thinking for "happy accidents" in the form of unexpected insights or test results that point to an entirely new avenue of investigation. Crucial discoveries, when they arrive, are almost always carried on the back of extraordinary labor. But the moment of their arrival, as in the case of Watson and Krick's discovery of the double-helix nature DNA, often seems to be a gift—a moment of inspiration and good luck. Handel described such an experience after a furious 23 days composing *Messiah*. "My eyes," he tearfully told his wife, "were opened to the glory of God." Mathematicians and physicists from Newton to Einstein to Hawking have recorded similar experiences of sudden, quantum leaps in their understanding and insight.

Knowledge leaves room for and values the serendipitous. Even while a company insists on its protocols and required programs, it holds them a bit suspect. In other words, a company leaves room for lightning to strike. Lacking such flexibility, an organization may find that great ideas and stunning insights flash upon the scene unnoticed, unappreciated, and unused.

3. *Knowledge can be owned.* In spite of high literacy rates in developed countries, most knowledge valuable for increasing wealth is privately held. Knowledge unrelated to the creation of wealth is freely available—at schools, for example—because it serves no one's specific interest or advantage in the marketplace. In other words, the works of Shakespeare are available to us all not because Shakespeare willed it so—he charged per view, so to speak, as co-owner of the Globe Theatre—but because since Shakespeare's death no one has built a substantial industry based on any kind of special or proprietary knowledge contained within his plays and poetry.

The same cannot be said for the knowledge necessary to make paint, preserve food safely, make or repair computers, or remove air pollution. These and countless other technologies and industrial functions are based on knowledge that is not made generally available. A company's "competitive advantage" often lies precisely in its privately held knowledge. Making paint may be easy, for all we in the general public know, but lacking the formula, we will continue to pay more for it per quart or liter than we pay for wine.

Several implications fan out from the notion of privately held knowledge. First, the identity of the owner must be clarified. Research and development personnel at computer, drug, cosmetic, and other similar companies routinely sign explicit and binding agreements with their employer that all knowledge accumulated, discovered, or developed during or as a result of their employment remains the sole possession of the employer. No matter how careful the wording of ownership agreements, of course, truly advantageous knowledge often has a way of getting out, usually with devastating results in the marketplace. Netscape's virtual ownership of internet browsing technologies, for example, was closely imitated—some would say stolen—by Microsoft, with substantial market losses to Netscape. The "best practice" in knowledge management for an organization is to determine what knowledge should be privately held and how it can be protected from competitors and clients.

Modern organizations find unique ways to pierce the shield of privately held knowledge. In many industries, companies acquire proprietary knowledge through friendly or hostile acquisitions or hiring away key employees. "Reverse engineering" of a competitor's products is another common way of obtaining otherwise propriety knowledge. Companies do so with the often-cynical strategy that legal challenges will take years to resolve in the courts—years during which the war for market share and profitability will be won. Ultimately, the issue of who owned what knowledge will often turn out to be financially moot.

4. *Knowledge is immanent as well as extant.* Not all knowledge worth managing in an organization is explicit and visible. Much organizational knowledge is held in creative reserve in the form of human resources and computer expert systems. Companies often test such knowledge by means of hypothetical scenarios, as in the case of Chevron's fortuitous testing of what it might do if Iraq ever invaded Kuwait. This immanent and preformed/pretested knowledge has the potential for becoming extant and formed at any moment required by the company, just as the energy within a battery can be tapped when needed.

A brain surgeon's expertise and capacity for action is an example of immanent knowledge. After years of study and practice, few brain surgeons can list the items within their knowledge base. The core competencies of brain surgeons—deep wells of insight, reflection, memory, and intuition—are forms of "knowledge in waiting" for times when they may be turned into action. Similar knowledge banks are in the minds of virtually all personnel who exercise creative thinking functions within an organization.

But just as brain surgeons must work to maintain and improve their immanent (that is, potential) knowledge base, organizations need to encourage and incentivize employees to "know" before they have to "go." This prospect forces us to confront difficult questions: How does a company go about nurturing immanent knowledge that may appear to have no direct application to "today's challenges" in the firm? How does a firm define the kinds of immanent knowledge that are worth investing in, and which are simply expensive flights of fancy that may never be of benefit to the company? Knowledge management requires a thorough discussion of these issues. No two companies will come up with the same options in such discussions, but lacking attention to these problems will assure that creative innovation is missing-in-action just when the firm needs it most.

5. *Knowledge can be stored.* It can safely be estimated that more knowledge has been externalized (that is, made observable and preservable) in the last two decades than in the entire previous history of mankind. On paper, film, tape, and above all by electronic storage means we have "lent out our minds," in the poet Milton's phrase. For example, 50,000 new sites *per week* continue to appear on the internet world-wide.

But now that we have so energetically externalized knowledge, we face an unexpected and ironic problem: how to internalize knowledge again. Getting knowledge out of our heads and onto disks, storage blades, or even paper was a feat of technology. Getting facts back into our heads for practical and creative use involves much more than technology.

For companies, the central intellectual work of the 21st century—true knowledge management deserving of the name—may lie not so much in accumulating externalized knowledge by purchasing massive databases and so forth as in developing time-efficient ways to process selected portions of that knowledge through a special chip whose essential circuits have not changed for thousands of years: the chip between our ears. Real-time internalization of knowledge for personnel may be a company's most imposing challenge. A training video or self-paced computer-learning program, for example cannot by internalized by the human mind using a "fast-forward" technique. The stored knowledge present on the video or computer program must be dealt out to the learner in real time, which does not vary substantially from individual to individual. (In other words, one employee does not master the contents of training program in one minute while it takes six hours for others to do so.)

The most poignant example of the dilemma of how to internalize knowledge lies in the efforts of elementary and secondary schools around the world to "get wired" to the internet and thereby enhance the availability of externalized knowledge for their students. But when well-intentioned teachers (or company trainers) advise students to search beyond Wikipedia on topics of interest, both instructors and students quickly confront the chaos of knowledge that now characterizes the internet. (The internet may rightly be called "the universal mind," but an argument can be made that it is simultaneously the mind of a madman.) A young student interested in using Google to search for information on goldfish was confounded and discouraged to confront more than 800,000 "hits" for the search term. The child asked his teacher, "Now what?" Where does one begin to make sense, much less useful progress, out of a vast knowledge base that lacks heuristics (familiar paths of inquiry) congenial to human learning and memory? Companies face the same dilemma: what meta-level of knowledge management could be provided to convert the micro-level of millions of factoids into real-time information that an employee can trust and use?

The immediate challenge facing the internet, as a global phenomenon, is to prevent cancerous growth—that is, wildly accretive expansion without regard for internal organization, external validation, or adaptation to the needs of the user. Paradoxically, we can access the internet faster than ever before only to find, once we get there, that the pages of the 'net are slower than ever in divulging the information we seek. Companies of all kinds have resorted to proprietary knowledge bases and search engines to address this dilemma. In general, we now face that reality that knowledge management is impossible apart from a system of organization (or selection) that makes knowledge accessible and useful in real time for real human beings.

Portions of this chapter adapted from *Measuring and Managing Knowledge* (2001), by Arthur Bell and Thomas Housel. McGraw-Hill/Irwin, by permission.

Chapter 16

Making Benchmarking a Reality in Your Organization

It is not difficult to conduct benchmarking so that the process yields valuable results—indeed, this book has been written to enable you to do so—but it takes careful planning in advance. By beginning the benchmarking process with thoughtful preparation, your chances for success will be maximized. Such planning should address the composition of the team, the resources given to them for their work, the framing or "mandate" of the benchmarking exercise within the organization, and the monitoring and sharing of their results.

For example, consider the first item listed, the composition of the bench-marking team—Who is on the team? Why? How much do they know about the techniques of benchmarking? What is their attitude toward the work assigned to them? Are incentives in place to reward them for a job well-done? Have you made provisions for mid-stream monitoring of the benchmarking process? Does your benchmarking team feel comfortable coming to you or others with problems they encounter, urgent discoveries that need addressing, or simple encouragement? Above all, can individual team members come to you to discuss difficult problems and conflicts occurring with the team itself?

When an organization is large enough to encompass several divisions (Human Resources, Research & Development, Production, Marketing, and so forth), it is almost always advantageous to build a benchmarking team comprised of complementary rather than overlapping talents. A well-chosen team also will represent diverse perspectives. Although five engineers (let's say) may see eye-to-eye from the beginning of the benchmarking effort and get the job "done" in record time, they more likely have succumbed to "groupthink" that prevents them from seeing important benchmarking issues. By contrast, an HR member of the team may pick up on motivational or attitudinal aspects of benchmarked examples—aspects that may determine the degree to which the company appreciates and makes use of the results of benchmarking. Similarly, a Marketing member of the team may counteract the "manufacturing mindset" among some other members, reminding them that data on what other *built* is not the same as data on what others *sold*.

Regardless of whether they are large or small, organizations can also use evaluative instruments such as the Myers-Briggs Type Inventory (MBTI) to ensure that their benchmarking teams are comprised of complementary perspectives. This validated tool defines in sixteen categories basic "habits of mind" for participants—that is, their basic tendencies in a variety of business-oriented, decision making situations. Reviewing the results of the MBTI can give a manager a good idea of which members will tend to see the "big picture;" which will focus on planning to the exclusion of creativity; which will rely on "group think" for formation and validation of their ideas; and which will insist on rationality to the exclusion of intuition. A manager forming a benchmarking team will find no perfect member for that group. Instead, he or she will find advantageous chemistry among group members—chemistry calculated to see benchmarking issues and problems in all their aspects and complexity.

Budgets in terms of human talent and money also matter from the outset of any benchmarking effort. It's important to decide how much effort you want to, and realistically can, devote to benchmarking. Xerox and Ford (see Appendices A and B) have devoted many millions of dollars to their efforts, while many other companies have gotten valuable results from the efforts of a few people over a couple of months. You must decide which of three potential approaches to take:

> • Do a benchmarking analysis of a *portion* of the enterprise—an internal business, a function, or one aspect of a business or function;

• Institute a company-wide benchmarking program, requiring all functions and groups to benchmark their activity, with adequate training to take on such a task;

• Use benchmarking more as a training tool or to achieve a change in "culture," encouraging all personnel to think competitively, but not asking them to produce any concrete benchmarking analysis. Participants will ask, 'What will our results be used for?' A manager can't reply, "Nothing." Instead, a company leader can make clear that self-study—Socrates' advice to "Know thyself"—is a first step toward more ambitious benchmarking at some point in the future.

Companies have reaped benefits from all three approaches; which approach you use depends upon your objectives and your resources.

In addition to choosing the right approach, you must apply the right resources. In almost all cases, the following guidelines will maximize your probability of success:

• The benchmarking analysis must be supported by high-level management, preferably in advance by their written and verbal communications with the workforce;

• Functional experts in the areas being benchmarked must participate and must earn the trust, through frequent contact and conversation, with other participants on the team;

• Analyst(s) need to be dedicated to the project for some period of time to get the work done. Their work cannot appear to be a "black box" into which the hard work of the benchmarking team is poured, with no idea of the outcome. Analysts must communicate their intentions and methods to the benchmarking team;

• You must budget time or money for collection of data from external sources including, in many cases, interviewing of outside sources. Top management must make clear to those who do such interviews that they are important contributors to the benchmarking process. Otherwise, members taken away from their usual work tasks may feel they are being taken off track with regard to performance goals and promotions.

You also must be sure that the analysis and its conclusions take the right form:

• The analysis should be tied to strategic considerations and not become a "mindless" numbers exercise. A good test of any chart, table, or graph is to require the analyst(s) to explain the meaning of that display to company members who haven't been privy to the terminology or methods of the analysis at hand.

• The analysis must conclude with concrete actions, plans, and targets. These "to-do" lists can be separated into long-term versus short-term goals or, alternately, into "aspirational" (that is, nice-to-have) versus "prompt fulfillment" goals (that is, must-have measures).

• The results of the analysis should be monitored over time to ensure accountability.

Finally, a certain type of "mindset" is crucial for successful benchmarking:

• Benchmarking analyses must be flexible. No two businesses or functions within your company should do benchmarking exactly the same way, because their industries, competitors, performance, and strategies are different. A company that produces a precise set of benchmarking forms to be filled out by every benchmarked business or function is on the wrong track. The goal of benchmarking is not to make sure that standard boxes are all checked. More important by far is the analysis that goes into which questions are posed for which benchmarked companies, and how their responses can shed light on ultimate benchmarking results.

- The premium must be on judgment_and_insight. The numbers and analysis won't give you the answer; they will point you towards it. A good benchmarking analysis will greatly enhance the quality of managers' judgment but it will not replace that judgment. In this regard, see the discussion of *interpretive* knowledge in Chapter 17.

- There must be a willingness to_estimate. Benchmarking (and competitive analysis or strategic planning in general, for that matter) is not a precise science. An "actionable" level of accuracy, rather than the "third decimal place," is the objective. Some benchmarking efforts have stalled or failed because analysts thought they shouldn't draw conclusions until they attained precision. One effective way to prevent "paralysis by analysis" is to follow the suggestions in Chapter 17 in forming a team made up of complementary tendencies and talents. Putting only number-crunchers on your benchmarking team will almost guarantee that the "third decimal place" issue will occupy far too much of their deliberations.

- Benchmarking must always be viewed as a means to an end. You don't study competitors because you're trying to learn about them; you study them because you're trying to learn what you should do differently. If you keep that in mind at all times, your analysis will be both more efficient and more effective. Throughout this process, it is wise neither to make gods nor devils of the competitors you are benchmarking. In almost all cases, you will discover things they do well and things they do poorly. Your goal is to "import the best and forget the rest."

The ultimate value of any benchmarking exercise is "what to do with the results". Obviously, the results and methodology are shared with those involved in the benchmarking. But an important key to benchmarking success is to have the team involved in implementation of study results. Team members can bring deep knowledge of the meaning of benchmarking results as well as a passion for their application to others in the company who did not participate directly in the benchmarking activity. Often, a different benchmarking team is selected for projects that suit them best within the company. Teams that come to their work with the head-start of in-depth knowledge of a particular aspect of the company can focus more quickly and accurately on what data to seek and the best sources for that data. These experienced teams also have increased credibility within the company when they take part—and often take the lead—in interpreting and implementing the results of their benchmarking work.

Companies must decide, often on a case-by-case basis, whether a benchmarking team should retain only its original members over a period of months or years, or whether new members should be cycled in, with an eye toward providing fresh perspective as well as continuity to later benchmarking projects in the company. A high-functioning benchmarking team operating under time constraints may resist having to bring new members "up to speed." On the other hand, a team that has fallen into the trap of "groupthink" may need new members to help it see data from new perspectives.

Ironically, even the best benchmarking teams sometimes forget to benchmark themselves—that is, conduct a post-mortem examination of how well they did their work, where and how it could be improved, and what advice they can share with other benchmarking groups within the organization. It remains a sound principle that a benchmarking project is not completed until a thorough post-mortem evaluation has been conducted.

Like anything else, benchmarking is a learning experience. If you keep these guidelines in mind, are willing to devote necessary time to the benchmarking process, and are willing to be creative in finding alternative ways to obtain and analyze data, you'll get through your first analysis successfully.

Having done that, you'll find the process infinitely easier – and even more rewarding – the next time around, and beyond.

Chapter 17

Reaching Conclusions about the Business through Benchmarking

Based on these sets of comparisons, most business management benchmarking efforts result in a number of different types of outputs.

First, competitive benchmarks are set that function as targets for managing the business. What level of service should we be able to maintain? At what prices and costs?

Second, many business management benchmarking efforts result in a Strategic or Business Plan for the function. These plans typically address issues such as what new customer sets might be targeted, what new services should be provided, what parts of the function would be better off outsourced, and what long-term trends must be planned for in advance. The concept of a Strategic Plan for an internal function is, to some companies, a surprising one, but those companies which have adopted this approach feel that it has been extremely valuable.

Finally, some business management benchmarking efforts actually include projected income statements and balance sheets for the newly-defined business. If your function doesn't actually charge a price to your internal customers, then the price is set as the cheapest available outside alternative. The cost of running the function is subtracted from price times volume, or revenue, in order to determine "income," and divided by the assets invested in the function to determine the return on assets. If the ROA is not satisfactory, then, as with any business, more work needs to be done to improve the function's competitive position. Internal units organized in this fashion are often called "profit centers," and are evaluated much as if they were stand-alone companies on their own.

Reaching conclusions about aspects of business through benchmarking depends, as we saw in Chapter 15, on accurate knowledge. Among the global companies that specialize in producing reliable knowledge are Bloomberg, S&P Global LL, J.D. Powers, and many others. But no matter how impressive the credentials of the knowledge provider are, a company must exercise *interpretive knowledge*, that is, data seen in the light of applicable meaning, before arriving at far-reaching conclusions about the business and its future direction.

An Example of the Interpretive Application of Knowledge

Any data set, whether gathered by the company itself or by an outside vendor, inevitably involves averaging instances or items across similar industries or circumstances. Based on such averages in the benchmarking process, a company makes decisions about its own decisions and expenditures: Are we paying too much? Should we negotiate for a better price or try for a prolonged period of time to lock in the present price we are paying? *Interpretive* knowledge adds an additional decision-making aspect to such considerations: *Are there local conditions that should be taken into account—conditions that are not reflected in the averaging methods of the data set upon which we are relying?*

An example of the application of such an interpretive knowledge tool in benchmarking is one of the most familiar supply chains in all societies, although often not recognized or analyzed as a supply chain: the transfer through stages of a young student through years of education toward eventual graduation and entry to the workforce. A primary driver of cost in this multi-year supply chain is the salary paid to faculty. Let's say, for example, that a freshman student aspires to enter the finance or accounting fields after graduation. A certain number of qualified instructors will have to be paid along the way to make that "supply chain" from freshman year through graduation successful.

Universities must hire and retain such qualified instructors—but at what cost in terms of salary and benefits? That economic factor will in large part determine how much tuition the student must pay and, in turn, influence how many students are able to apply for admission (the cost of tuition being the primary barrier to entry for many students). In this era when qualified faculty can teach virtually anywhere where their services are required, universities share information with one another (through such organizations in business as the Association to Advance Collegiate Schools of Business International [AACSB] and the Accreditation Board for Engineering and Technology [ABET]) about average salary and benefit packages offered to newly-minted PhDs seeking faculty positions.

Let's say, for purposes of illustration, that University A learns through its professional organization that the average starting salary for a new PhD in Finance within business schools in the U.S. is $120,000. Armed with this information, a Dean or other University administrator may feel confident in offering this approximate salary to job candidates.

It is precisely at this juncture that *interpretive* knowledge becomes of paramount importance. While a starting salary of $120,000 may be satisfactory to new Finance PhDs considering positions in the Southern or Midwestern states, that salary (even though it is the average of all comparable salaries for this position across the U.S.) may cause the "broken link" in the education supply chain in such cities as New York City and San Francisco.

In other words, broad-brush data from even the most reputable sources must be locally *interpreted* if it is to be meaningful in reaching the goal of successful hiring. In both New York City and San Francisco, among other "expensive cities," University administrators seeking to hire new faculty have become used to what they ruefully call "the fatal real estate drive." Even after a new faculty applicant has been duly impressed by his or her future colleagues, work conditions, teaching schedule, facilities, and so forth, there comes the so-called "fatal" moment (usually at the end of a candidate's hiring interviews) when he or she is driven around the city (in our case, New York City or San Francisco) to learn about typical rental or purchase prices for suitable lodging.

Suddenly, the $120,000 salary minus usual taxes of $40,000 pales in the harsh light of one-bedroom rentals that start at $4000 per month and unremarkable homes starting at $1,000,000 or more. As one Dean put it, "I could see the wheels turning inside my candidate's head: '$120,000 minus $40,000 taxes leaves $80,000 to spend on all other expenses. If a two-bedroom apartment in a safe neighborhood with good schools can't be found for less than $7,000 per month (as is the case in New York City and San Francisco), that's $84,000 devoted to housing alone! There's no way I can afford to take this job!'

Interpretive knowledge, often included under the broad category of "management by exception," means that data used for benchmarking must be evaluated (interpreted) in the light of local conditions—"local" referring at times to geographical factors but often more broadly to specific, "on-the-ground" circumstances. In our earlier case of New York City and San Francisco, this kind of *interpretive* knowledge means that the educational supply chain at schools such as Stanford and U.C. Berkeley necessitates starting salaries of $200,000 and above for new PhD job applicants in high-demand fields such as Finance, Accounting, and Computer Science. National averages for these salaries mean virtually nothing in hiring environments where housing costs play such a dominant role.

More broadly, the concept of *interpretive* knowledge should remind all organizations of the importance of seeking out, listening to, and acting on information that bubbles up to headquarters from branch locations. "Bubble up," in fact, is an inadequate metaphor, given the crucial value of local information. Organizations must plan for robust information pipelines that deliver local information accurately and often to headquarters or regional centers. Such local information dramatically influences the most basic business decisions, including the following:

- if we move company headquarters from an unattractive but affordable urban location to an attractive but expensive suburban location, what influence will this move have on employees who must relocate to the new location? Can we reasonably expect to keep salaries the same when the housing costs of employees will rise significantly?
- if we decentralize our workforce, can we depend on electronic meetings and other technological communication connections to replace the face-to-face work culture that has proven successful for the company in the past?
- if we accede to top management's desire to occupy posh new offices in a business tower instead of their present facilities within the factory, what hidden price will we pay for distancing company leadership from the rank-and file?

Benchmarking can help address these questions by offering parallel cases and consequences. But no gathering and analysis of similar cases can be said to be truly comparable to your local circumstances. The best benchmarking always includes the need for reflective, insightful use of local knowledge to interpret the meaning of data as it applies to your specific environment, not to broad averages of what others have experienced.

Positive examples of these kinds of interpreted outcomes of benchmarking can be found in Appendices A, B, and C. Appendix A tells the epic story of Ford's many benchmarking decisions in deciding if, how, and when to launch its Sable and Taurus models. Appendix B reveals how Xerox used benchmarking to re-visit its core values and revive its flagging stock. Appendix C shows how companies benchmarked their decisions on whether or to what extent to use outsourced customer call centers.

As these appendices demonstrate in detail, business management benchmarking in some ways can be the most revealing type of benchmarking of all, precisely because the functions benchmarked are rarely thought of in competitive or strategic terms. Successfully implemented, business management benchmarking can ensure that each function in your company is performing at "best-in-class" levels, significantly raising the odds that your company will be the leader in its competitive marketplace.

Appendix A

Ford's Taurus and Sable

Among the most dramatic examples of benchmarking success is Ford's development of the Taurus and Sable in 1986. These new cars won praise in the marketplace and achieved operating improvements such as a decline in the need for repairs after assembly from 10%-15% to only 1%. These gains were the direct result of a benchmarking process that also brought far-reaching changes in the company's organization and its competitive outlook.

Before the Taurus and Sable, Ford had been plagued by poor product quality. However, in the late 70s, Ford began to face the fact that its competitors were building better cars. "We finally realized that fuel economy wasn't the only reason that consumers were flocking to imports," said Ford's Chairman Donald E. Peterson.

Ford's second problem was organization. One of the biggest obstacles Ford had to overcome was convincing its personnel that the auto industry had become permanently more competitive. They needed to change their focus from internal goals (*e.g.*, "8% annual productivity gains") to external goals (*e.g.*, "the best productivity in the industry"). The company accomplished this by setting up a completely new organization to develop the Taurus/Sable. Management was given a clear slate and told to "build the best car in the world; how you build it doesn't matter."

How the Process Worked

Competitors were analyzed extensively to determine the optimal design for the Taurus and Sable. Ford defined 400 different areas important to the success of a car model. These included everything from braking to the heft of the ignition key. The company also examined other car companies' production and design methods in order to determine how it could improve costs.

Ford then chose a "best-in-class" competitor for each of the 400 areas. Engineers combed over 50 different mid-size car models, while staff teams traveled to Japan to learn Japanese production methods. The process was wrenching for the company: hardly any best-in-class models were Fords.

Based on this data, management then assigned responsibility to specific groups of people to meet or beat the best-in-class competitor in each area of performance. If this goal was not met, either an explanation of the failure or a timetable for meeting the goal was required. In this way, the company gave direct control over success or failure to those most closely involved with the product and had concrete measures to gauge their performance.

Results: Product Improvements

The results were impressive. At the time of the model introduction, Ford claimed to have met or beaten the best-in-class competitors in 77% of the defined areas. Three hundred features were "borrowed" from best-in-class competitors and incorporated into the car. For another 20% of the areas, Ford set a schedule to beat the best-in-class by 1988.

From a product standpoint, the Taurus/Sable model was soon a resounding success. The car received rave press reviews, and Ford soon had a five-month backlog of orders.

Results: Design Process Improvements

The design process was also improved significantly. In studying its competitors' approach to designing a product, Ford gained some valuable insight into how to streamline the process. In the past, Ford had designed cars in steps: product planners came up with a general concept; design teams gave it form; engineering developed specifications; and, finally, manufacturing and suppliers made the parts.

Now Ford adopted Japanese methods of automobile development. It brought representatives from planning, design, engineering, and manufacturing together at the initial stages in order to work out the bugs early. The company also signed long-term agreements with suppliers that allowed them to join in the design process to make sure component designs were compatible with manufacturing designs. This also enabled suppliers to make capital improvements based on the long-term value of the contract and thus to amortize their cost over a longer period. This process allowed Taurus to be designed with fewer problems and lower manufacturing costs. "We never (before) had the supplier input that we had on this car. Now we'll never do it any other way," said Lewis Veraldi, head of the Taurus Project.

Results: Manufacturing Improvements

Benchmarking also influenced the manufacturing process. After measuring the competition, Ford realized that its assembly costs were much too high. The company took a number of ideas from its rivals, such as actively soliciting suggestions from assembly line workers. Suggestions such as using the same head size on all bolts and making body panels from just 2 parts instead of 6 greatly improved productivity. For the first time, foremen were allowed to deal directly with suppliers, shortening the line of communication when there was a problem on the line. Workers were allowed to stop the line at any time, allowing them time to correctly install all parts. And the assembly process itself was changed. For example, Ford now runs a separate trim line for car doors, allowing more efficient assembly of both the doors and the cars.

Finally, Ford sliced the option list from 180 to 37, thus limiting the chance for assembly glitches and allowing lot sizes to rise from 1,000 to 13,000 cars. As a result of these changes:

> • Cars were now built with only 24.5 man-hours/car, the best ratio for any American mid-size car operation.

● Fewer than one car per hundred had to go back for repairs after final assembly, 10-15 times better than 5 years ago. Quality Assurance Director John Monoogian said, "If 10 years ago they had heard of our repair rate targets, they would have laughed."

Ford's Philosophy of Benchmarking

For Ford, the impact of benchmarking reached far beyond an individual product and became a means of changing the organizational culture. Ford made a conscious effort to change the "mind-set" of senior management from being only "bottom-line-results-oriented" to also becoming "process-driven."

Ford's success is attributable to its high level of commitment to the process and also to the fact that it didn't view benchmarking as a "copy-cat" or "catch-up" exercise. Said Veraldi, "The important thing is not to aim to be as good as your competition. If you do, then by the time your product is out, your competition may be ahead again. You have to strive to be <u>better</u> than the BICs (Best-in-Class)."

The Future of Benchmarking at Ford

Although it had yielded significant results, the benchmarking process was just beginning at Ford. Ford now views the analysis of competitors as an ongoing process, acknowledging that there is a continuous need for improvement. Top management has been so pleased with the results that the Taurus project was made the blueprint for all future projects. Lewis Veraldi, head of the Taurus Team, was promoted to Vice President of Car Operations with the responsibility of spreading the philosophy throughout the company.

In 1989, Ford extended its benchmarking to a best practice program that was shared company-wide in the mid-1990s. Best Practice Replication was started by Dale McKeehan, the former general manager of vehicle operations at Ford. It involved every plant with the mission of driving productivity improvements. The key to its success was measuring the value of the knowledge transferred between internal groups and the resulting replication of best practices across these groups. It consisted of three fundamental steps:

- Step 1: Collect proven practices – look for "gems" for replication by each community gatekeeper

- Step 2: Communicate the practices – share and notify others about the findings of Step 1

- Step 3: Manage the process: report back to others on intent, and disposition, then collect and report on the number of replications, plus, most importantly, recognize results

"What we could have done better, and will next time," said Veraldi, "is to expand our horizon. We need to look at all kinds of cars, not just mid-size ones. Even beyond that, we need to look at totally different industries, such as how airplane seats are made and how trucking companies implement their distribution systems." Ford's recent success relative to General Motors and Chrysler can be attributed to such far-reaching and external-based thinking, brought about by the benchmarking process.

Appendix B

Benchmarking at Xerox

Years earlier, Xerox embarked upon a similar pioneering benchmark effort that was applied to all functional areas across the company.

The process was initially motivated by a sharp decline in market share. Xerox invented the first photocopier in 1959 and essentially maintained a virtual worldwide monopoly in the copier market throughout the 60s and early 70s. The company dictated to its customers and ignored emerging competition. From 1976 to 1981, however, Xerox's market share plummeted from 82% to 35%. IBM and Kodak had developed high-end machines, while Japanese competitors, primarily Canon and Savin, had come to dominate the low-end. Xerox's product development function had caught the "disease of creeping elegance" -- while Xerox was busy building the most advanced copiers in the world, its competition was building the products that customers wanted: low-cost, reliable machines.

How Benchmarking was Envisioned

Benchmarking was viewed as a tool to "teach Xerox how to compete," Charles Christ, Vice President of Copier Manufacturing, remarked:

"Our costs were not only way out in left field, they weren't even in the ball park. We were horrified to find that the Japanese were selling their machines at what it cost us to make ours. We had to aspire to world-class benchmarks in every aspect of our business. We had to develop an external focus instead of an internal one. Up to that time, we had been putting in 8% productivity gains each year, which we thought was pretty good. But we had been benchmarking against ourselves. We weren't looking outside."

How Benchmarking Works at Xerox

All parts of the organization participate in Xerox's benchmarking program. Responsibility is shared by all functional areas and is fully supported and driven by top management.

The productivity, cost, and quality of virtually every function and task -- from inventory levels to the number of drawings a design engineer turns out in a year -- is compared with either the competition or the company that is considered best in the area. As an example of the latter, L.L, Bean was the company against which Xerox benchmarked its order processing and warehousing functions. Bob Camp, Distribution Manager, said, "I think we learned a lot from Bean. It really shows the nature of benchmarking. In a lot of ways, it is like a dog-breeding competition. We're looking for the best of the breed for a particular business practice even if the company has nothing to do with copiers."

A wide range of "benchmarks" was established. Some diverse examples include:

- Cost of a function (sales, service, distribution, etc.) as a percent of revenues

- Labor overhead rate

- Cost per page of publication

- Number of problem-free machines

- Billing error rate

- Service response time

The process initially met with resistance. Paul Regensburger, Benchmarking Manager, said, "When you come back from Japan and tell someone they have a 50% problem in cost, they tend to be defensive. We like to say there are phases to the implementation of benchmarking, based on people's reactions. The first is...they don't believe it. The second is (dismay). Then frustration. And, finally, action. That's the good phase, when the ball starts to roll."

Results of Benchmarking

From a low of 35%, Xerox's market share climbed back to about 45%. Many strategic and tactical changes were made, *e.g.*:

- The company reduced the number of suppliers to 300 from 5,000 to be able to work more closely with them;

- Each product development group now has input from design, manufacturing and service engineers from the very beginning of a project ("simultaneous engineering");

- Xerox learned from the Japanese not to re-invent the wheel every time around; only 30%-40% of the components in its new model were unique to that machine, compared with 80% in the past;

- Much of the Xerox bureaucracy is gone, replaced by entrepreneurial "product development," "crisis," and "problem-solving" teams.

Productivity improvements, according to Xerox, have been dramatic:

- Manufacturing costs were cut in half;

- Development time was cut by two-thirds;

- Quality problems were cut by two-thirds;

- The company increased its volume with only half of the direct labor and about 35% of the corporate staff employed in 1980.

As one unexpected side benefit of benchmarking, the company realized that it was the lowest-cost producer of photoreceptors. As a result of that discovery, Xerox began selling replacement photoreceptors for Savin and Royal copiers.

The company, however, acknowledges that it still has a way to go to meet the best-in-class.

- Xerox reduced its parts rejection rate from 8,000/million to 1,300/million, but the Japanese are under 1,000.

- The company's costs still are not low enough to compete in the market for low-end copiers.

The bottom line, though, is that Xerox believes that it would not be in the copier business today without benchmarking.

Summing up the corporate reaction to benchmarking, David T. Kearns, Chairman and CEO said, "We have come far enough to know that we can continue to manufacture a significant part of our machines in the United States and compete on a worldwide basis."

The Future of Benchmarking at Xerox

Xerox is by no means through with benchmarking. It is counting on the process to produce even greater improvements in the future. According to Lyndon Haddon of Xerox, "Where companies go wrong is that they don't start benchmarking <u>before</u> they're threatened. Also companies tend to start and then quit when they feel they have gotten where they want to be. Actually, this is an ongoing process that you should never stop,"

Today, Xerox sees that one of the key metrics is the pace of innovation. As George Gibson, LSS Black Belt, Xerox Research Center Webster says "It would be impossible to keep up the required pace of innovation if you tried to do everything yourself. So how do you keep from crossing lines as you form multiple networks for innovation? That is something we spend a fair amount of time on." As a global organization, Xerox works to enable geographically dispersed teams and involve even those who would not conventionally be considered. In the past, Xerox's central engineering center would dictate how IT would be leveraged to support collaboration. Now, there is no central authority to enforce the use of collaboration tools. A number of tools and technologies are centrally funded and provided to employees to use as they see fit—that is, they are centrally coordinated but locally controlled. Serious accounting issues in 2000 caused a major internal crisis, but it allowed the company to eliminate many of the traditional silos with Xerox. The consequence has been that today Xerox can far better focus on customers and drivers of change in the external market across its broad organization.

Appendix C

Decisions about Internal Customer Call Centers

Following the collapse of the computer bubble in the late 1990s, new off-shore service firms in India started to appear, utilizing high-speed global telecommunication network, which, thanks to the bursting of the bubble had suddenly become significantly cheaper. One of the new services these firms offered was outsourced customer call centers. In the early 2000s, an increasing number of firms in high-cost English speaking countries, like the U.S. and the U.K., began to use these services and close their internal call centers as there appeared to be major cost benefits.

However, some ten years later, it was apparent that many customers were not happy with the quality of these offshore services as they were managed by individuals whose English skills were less than ideal. With customer complaints increasing a large multinational decided to review its policy of only using offshore call centers. To begin with it began by interviewing internal groups (customers) who were being served by its call centers to get their views of how well these centers fulfilled their needs. It learned, to its surprise, that some had stopped offshoring their call centers to India and were using local U.S.-based outsourced call center services, while others were quite happy.

By correlating these results with internal customers' responses, a wide range of conclusions were reached. A sample of these conclusions include:

- Customers were using U.S. base service where high touch customer service was essential to maintaining customer satisfaction.

- Indian service was being used where cost was a major consideration rather than concerns around customer satisfaction.

- There were major differences between Indian service centers, and quality could be significantly improved by working with the right Indian firm and building a close working relationship to understand their recruiting and training programs.

- Domestic U.S.-based call centers were aggressively looking to complete against offshorers and very competitive deals could be struck to cover specific areas of operation.

- As telecommunication technology increased in sophistication, it was increasingly possible to use both India and U.S. based services, switching callers between them to minimize dissatisfaction when problems occurred, and even to bring some of the call volume to in-house experts rather than external support teams.

Based on these insights, the organization took a series of actions to develop new corporate guidelines on managing customer service and how to contract for external call centers. After these changes were implemented, the use of U.S.-based call centers increased significantly, as did the overall customer satisfaction in those groups that made the switch. At the same time, a repeat survey a year later revealed that customers were far happier than in the past and felt they were getting better service at a more reasonable price.

Appendix D

Essentials of Business Model Benchmarking

A growing number of companies are using benchmarking to define and manage business_areas which were previously thought of as internal "activities" or internal "functions." Benchmarking is a way to measure those functions relative to best-in-class companies and customers' needs, in order to determine if they are being managed as well and as profitably as possible.

Business management benchmarking has been applied to many different types of internally focused functions. Examples include:

- The reprographics department

- Library services

- In-plant or in-building utilities

  - Purchasing and support of personal computers, telecommunications systems, and office automation

  - Support of Internet and mobile systems

  - Data security

  - Data centers

  - Warehousing

  - In-house laboratories

  - Public relations

Business management benchmarking usually includes four steps:

- Defining the business and the customer set;

- Identifying best-in-class competitors;

- Comparing your performance to the best-in-class;

- Reaching conclusions about the business.

Each of these steps is described below.

Defining the Business and the Customer Set

Often, it is not obvious what business the activity is in and what customers it serves. For example, is the goal of the library services group to be a repository for in-house information, or to help employees find whatever they need in-house or outside? Is the purpose of the office automation support group to buy equipment on behalf of users, train users, service the equipment, or all of the above?

There is also often internal debate concerning the identity of the customer set: which organizations and types of employees is the function supposed to serve, and how should it prioritize their needs? Regardless of the outcome of that debate, managers , always note that the business management benchmarking process helps their group realize that they do have "customers" (even if they're internal customers), and they must keep those customers satisfied if they want to stay in business.

Identifying Best-in-Class Competitors

For business management benchmarking, there are almost always two sets of best-in-class competitors.

The first group are potential "outsource" competitors. The IT group within your organization must compare its performance to companies on the outside that could write much of the code for new and upgrades to your computer software, or use external telephone support services for your customer call centers. No matter how accustomed the company is to having a function performed internally, there are almost always outside alternatives and they need to be evaluated in terms of the service and quality they provide relative to what your organization can deliver by resourcing them internally.

The second set of best-in-class companies are called "parallel companies." These are other organizations similar in size and purpose to your own. For example, one large company with an internal laboratory compared it to the internal labs of five other large companies in the same or similar industries. This "parallel company" data helps provide perspective on how other organizations attack the problems which your function faces.

Comparing Your Performance to the Best-in-Class

Three types of comparisons to the best-in-class companies are typically made. First, the quality or level of service provided is compared. The question here is: is our function providing the same amount of support as the best-in-class? Components of this question include:

- Are we offering the same range of services?

- Are they being delivered with comparable quality, or by comparably skilled people?

- Are they being delivered in as timely a fashion?

- Is the customer able to pick and choose, or "unbundle" the services we offer?

Secondly, the *prices* of the outsource companies should be compared to your prices. Can outside copying firms, security services, or warehouses supply the services we offer for less than what we charge our internal customers? If so, by how much, and for which services?

If you actually charge your internal customers for your services (as many functions do), this analysis is relatively straightforward. If you do not, then an "effective" price must be imputed. To calculate a price, you must include your costs *and* a fair return on any assets invested in the function. Comparing your costs to the outside suppliers' prices gives you an unfair advantage and will often yield the wrong result.

Third, your company's *costs* should be compared to those of both the parallel and the outsource companies at a fairly detailed level, if possible. Whereas comparing prices will tell you if you're competitive, comparing costs will tell you *why* you're competitive or *why you're not*. Cost comparisons typically include headcount and salaries for various personnel categories, as well as a number of different types of non-people costs. Additional research on the methods and processes of the best-in-class will reveal how they achieve lower cost in certain areas.

Index

www.ingramcontent.com/pod-product-compliance
Lightning Source LLC
Chambersburg PA
CBHW051409200326
41520CB00023B/7167